Alex Byrne

Practical Accounts and Bookkeeping

In easy steps is an imprint of In Easy Steps Limited
4 Chapel Court · 42 Holly Walk · Leamington Spa
Warwickshire · United Kingdom · CV32 4YS
www.ineasysteps.com

Notice of Liability
Every effort has been made to ensure that this book contains accurate
and current information. However, In Easy Steps Limited and the
author shall not be liable for any loss or damage suffered by readers
as a result of any information contained herein.

Trademarks
All trademarks are acknowledged as belonging to their respective
companies.

In Easy Steps Limited supports The Forest Stewardship Council (FSC),
the leading international forest certification organisation. All our titles
that are printed on Greenpeace approved FSC certified paper carry the
FSC logo.

MIX
Paper from
responsible sources
FSC
www.fsc.org   FSC® C020837

Printed and bound in the United Kingdom

ISBN 978-1-84078-418-3

Contents

1 Introduction

You will be surprised how often you might need your business accounts

Business Accounts

Hot tip

What a limited company can or cannot do is set out in the Articles of Association which are produced when a company is registered. The Articles are commonly very wide ranging and it is unlikely that the activities of the company will be restricted by them. However, all company directors should know what they say.

Beware

Shareholder Directors of limited companies and members of LLP's can be held responsible for the debts of limited companies/LLP's if they are guilty of fraud or wrongful trading. (knowing they traded while unable to pay the debts of the business as they become due).

Businesses can be sole traders, partnerships, companies or limited liability partnerships.

- **A SOLE TRADER** is a self-employed individual who is personally financially responsible if things go wrong e.g. if the business cannot pay its debts and taxes, the individual's home or other assets may be at risk

- **A PARTNERSHIP** is more than one self-employed person working together to make a profit and sharing everything on an agreed split. Each partner is personally responsible for all debts run up by the partnership as a whole except for tax debts (individuals are responsible for their own tax debts). Again their homes or other assets may be at risk

- **A LIMITED COMPANY** is a separate legal structure where the liability of owners of the business is limited to the amount of their shares. Any legal action has to be against the Company not the shareholders and the shareholders' personal assets are often safe.

- **A LIMITED LIABILITY PARTNERSHIP (LLP)** has many of the features of a normal partnership - but it is also like a limited company in that members in an LLP cannot usually lose more than they invest.

"Business" is the same as "trade". Being "self-employed" means you are your own boss and answer only to yourself. The word "firm" is often used to describe a partnership. The expression "my company" is commonly used to mean any business whether a company or a sole trader or partnership.

You may hear the expression "profession" which describes people who do jobs which need special training and skill and often involve a high level of education, such as doctors or lawyers. Professional people may be self-employed as sole traders (for example as Consultants) or be Limited Companies or Limited Liability Partnerships although sometimes the rules of their governing organisation prevent them being anything other than sole traders.

However you run your business, you need to prepare accounts.

9

What are Accounts?

Accounts are a **summary** of the business financial activities for a period of time, commonly 12 months. They can also be referred to as financial statements.

Why does a business need accounts?

● **To know how the business is doing...**

Why not just look at how much money you have in the bank?

The bank balance does not show you who owes you and who you owe.

For example, say you have a warehouse selling clothes to shops and other retailers and you sell £58,000 worth of clothes, on credit (i.e. customers do not pay for them when they take them but agree to pay later), so your Sales are £58,000.

You owe your suppliers , who you bought the clothes from, £16,000, so purchases are £16,000.

You have made a profit of £42,000 (Goods sold £58,000 less goods purchased £16,000):

		£
Clothes sold on credit	(Sales)	58000
Clothes bought on credit	(Purchases)	16000
	Profit	42000

but you have no money in your bank account:

	£
Money received for Sales and paid into the bank	0
Money paid out of the bank for Purchases	0
Bank transactions	None
Money in bank	0

The bank account does not show any of these transactions because they are not yet paid for, so relying on your bank account and the bank balance alone would not help you see how the business was doing **at all**.

To raise money for the business e.g. bank loan/overdraft

The bank will ask you for your latest accounts to see if you can afford to pay the loan/overdraft back as well as the interest on the loan. People often complain that banks offer loans to people who already have money e.g. savings, but are not so keen to lend businesses money when they first start out or want to expand. In other words the bank wants a safe bet that it's loan will be repaid.

The bank almost always is only interested in a business which has been trading successfully for a while and has a good track record, and it wants to see the business accounts before it will consider lending. Often the bank will want a lot more e.g. cashflow forecasts and possibly management accounts.

To raise money for the owner(s) e.g. a mortgage to buy a home

Again the bank or building society will want to know the businessman or woman can afford the mortgage repayments on their earnings and their accounts will be an indication of this.

For an insurance claim

It may be that the business is insured for loss of sales or profits in the event of a fire or flood, for example. In the event of a claim, the Insurance Company might want to see the accounts to see what the Sales and Profits have been in previous years to check that the insurance claim is reasonable (they may also wish to check the records to see what the sales were in the same months in previous years).

For making a business tax return

A Sole Trader or Partnership pays tax AND national insurance on the business profits. The accounts show the Profit, which often has to be adjusted to arrive at the Profit for tax purposes.

For partners in a partnership to see their share of the business

Partners may lend money to the partnership, will take money out of the business to live on, and may be entitled to different

Hot tip

Get your accounts done as soon as possible so they are available when you need them and so the figures are as up-to-date as they can be and therefore most useful.

11

shares of the profits each year depending on what has been agreed. The accounts will keep track of each partner's share of the business.

- **For a business which is a company, for filing with Companies House**

  Companies have to file accounts with Companies House every year. Sometimes the accounts for Companies House are for a different period than the accounts for tax for HM Revenue & Customs and so it is important to align them early or the business is faced with paying for two different sets of accounts each year!

- **To sell the business**

  The purchaser's accountant will want to see how the business has been doing to see if it is worth the price that is being asked for it. He will ask for copies of accounts for the last few years.

Does a Business Need an Accountant?

A bank or building society lending money will always want the accounts to have been prepared by a qualified, independent accountant who does not work for the business.

Many lenders may ask for copies of tax returns if the businessman is a sole trader or partnership as their tax returns show the accounts figures, provided the tax returns have been prepared by qualified accountants.

HM Revenue & Customs expect profits of a business to be calculated using current accepted accountancy principles. If a business can familiarise itself with all of these and all the tax rules, then in theory a business does not need an accountant. However, HMRC are more likely to challenge a tax return received from a business without an accountant because it is more likely to be wrong.

Tax rules are complicated and a business may be able to reduce its tax bill by being advised by a suitably qualified accountant. Equally a business may be paying too little tax because of ignorance and should HMRC discover this, they will raise extra tax bills going back up to 6 years AND charge interest and penalties. In some cases they will go back 20 years!

HMRC can charge penalties even though errors may be innocent because they expect businesses to take reasonable care in completing their tax returns. They may not regard the business as having taken reasonable care if it did not use the services of a suitably qualified accountant.

If the business did not use an accountant, HMRC would expect it to seek professional advice on any potential tax issues. It would not be enough for the business to say that it was not aware that it had any!

Very large businesses need to have their accounts audited. Their business records and accounts have to be checked by an independent accountant qualified to carry out audits. The auditor will say whether he feels that the accounts and other financial statements accurately and fairly represent the business's financial position. Accounts for small and medium businesses do not need to be audited.

Beware

HMRC do not accept ignorance as an excuse.

Summary

- Accounts or financial statements are a summary of the business finances usually for 12 months

- They are used:

    - to see how the business is doing

    - where more than one person is running the business, to show their stake in the business

    - to raise money

    - for insurance

    - for tax returns

    - for Companies House if the business is a company

    - for selling the business

    So Accounts are useful for a variety of purposes and are not just for tax

- A business may need to prepare **different types of financial statements** e.g. annual accounts, management accounts, and cashflow statements and forecasts

- Using a qualified accountant should give you accurate accounts, help you raise money, reduce your tax bill and stay out of trouble with HMRC

2 Annual Accounts

Anyone can put together simple accounts

Basic Annual Accounts

How are accounts prepared?

In order to prepare annual accounts you need to record all transactions in your business.

Basic records you need to prepare accounts

Sales invoices, bills & receipts

"Invoices" and "bills" are the same thing. People will ask for an invoice or bill when buying goods or services and will give an invoice or bill when selling goods or services. They are pieces of paper (or electronic record) to document the supply of goods or services whether for immediate payment or for payment later (on credit). Invoices should list the goods or services, and the buyers and sellers.

Receipts are usually a receipt for the payment for goods or services such as a till receipt or a receipt for something paid for in cash.

Invoices, bills and receipts are the prime records of trading transactions.

The accounts for a period (normally for 12 months) need to include all invoices, bills and receipts **dated in that period.**

These are all you need to prepare the simplest set of accounts often called a Statement of Income & Expenses (or Profit & Loss account). The Profit & Loss Account shows whether the Sales of the business are more than its Expenses and it has made a profit, or its Expenses are more than its Sales and it has made a loss.

EXCEPTIONALLY accounts can be prepared from estimated figures without records e.g. where records have been destroyed and cannot be reconstituted or have never been kept.

16

Profit & Loss Account

Statement of Income & Expenses (or Profit & Loss Account)

The most important question to ask and focus on when keeping records and preparing annual accounts is – **what period are the accounts going to cover?** You should only include invoices, bills, receipts, till print-outs, etc, **that apply to that period.**

Example of a simple Profit & Loss Account:

Year Ended 31st March		
Profit & Loss Account	**£**	**£**
Income		58000
Sales (or Work Done)		
Less Expenses		
Materials Purchased	16000	
Wages	8000	
Premises	2500	
Repairs & Maintenance	500	
Motor	2000	
Office or Administration	1500	
Advertising	2000	
Accountancy	500	33000
Profit		**25000**

The figures in the Profit & Loss Account are the total of all the pieces of paper i.e. invoices, bills and receipts, dated in the period covered by the accounts.

Sales are the total of all the invoices issued by a business to its customers. If the business is, for example, a shop or a pub where Sales are rung up on a till, Sales will be a total of all the till print-outs often referred to as "Takings" (although in the accounts they will almost certainly still be called "Sales"). In those sorts of business, the till print-outs instead of invoices act as the record of Sales.

...cont'd

The word "Sales" is often used to describe all types of business income from shop sales to the work done by say a builder. Sometimes instead of "Sales" the expression "Work Done" is used or just "Income".

In the Profit and Loss on the previous page, if all the Customers paid for their Sales and the business paid all its expenses i.e. nothing was on credit, then the business would have £25,000 i.e. the amount of the Profit.

These are the basic annual accounts your business needs.

However, for a complete set of accounts, most businesses also prepare a **Balance Sheet**. This is covered in detail in the next chapter, Chapter 3.

Profit & Loss Account is often referred to as just **Profit & Loss**, or even abbreviated to **P & L**. In this book, we have used any one of these phrases depending on space and for ease of reading. Similarly, Balance Sheet is often referred to as just **BS**.

JANUARY FEBRUARY
MARCH APRIL MAY
JUNE JULY AUGUST
SEPTEMBER OCTOBER
NOVEMBER DECEMBER

Your annual accounts can cover any 12 month period but it is more convenient if they run to the end of a month.

You can prepare your accounts for any 12 month period. In the first year if you start your business on say the 15th October, then strictly your first year's accounts will be 15th October to 14th October in the following year.

However, this can be confusing and it is easier for your first accounts to be for the period 15th October to say 30th September in the following year. Although this is only 351 days (365 less the 14 days from 1st Oct to 14th Oct), it means that all your accounts after your first accounts can be for 12 months and can finish at the end of the month.

If you started on say 15th of October, for a small business it would not be the end of the world if you made your first "year" 1st October to 30th September even though nothing really happened from 1st October to 15th October.

Summary

- The Profit & Loss Account gives limited information. It tells you what the business has earned, what sort of expenses it has had, and the profit (or loss) it has made

- It does not tell you:

  – How much you have in the bank

  – How much is owed to you

  – How much you owe

  – The value of vehicles, equipment, etc that you have

  – Whether you have any loans or HP outstanding

- It will not tell you whether there is anything left of the profit the business has made over the years after the money you have taken for yourself

- The single most important question about records and accounts is what is the period covered by the accounts

- The minimum records that you need to keep for your accounts are invoices, bills and receipts

- If you do not keep records, you could be fined by HMRC

- The Profit & Loss Account gives you minimum information. For more complete information, you will need more records and a Balance Sheet

- A full set of accounts comprises a Profit & Loss AND a **Balance Sheet**

3 Balance Sheet

A Balance Sheet is a guide to what the business is worth

Don't forget

Make sure that your accounts give you sufficient information to see not only how the business did but what state it is in i.e. that as well as a Profit & Loss, you have a Balance Sheet.

What is a Balance Sheet?

It is a snapshot of what the business is worth on any given day. It is a list of the various business assets and liabilities at close of business on that day.

What are Assets and Liabilities?

- Assets are things of value belonging to the business

- Liabilities are things that the business owes

Money owed by **customers** to the business for goods or services they have bought are debts and the customers are **debtors.** Although the business does not have the money owed to it yet, it expects to get it and so debtors have value and are Assets.

Similarly **suppliers** owed money by the business are **creditors** and this money will have to be paid by the business at some time in the future and so is a Liability of the business.

Assets less Liabilities gives the worth of the business or Net Assets.

If the business sold off (or realised) all its assets (including collecting the money owed to the business i.e. from its debtors) and paid off all its liabilities (including paying everyone the business owed, i.e. its creditors), it would be left with a pile of money and this would be the value of the business (with one exception – see Goodwill below).

Each figure on the Balance Sheet is the total of all the transactions for that item in the period covered by the accounts, often 12 months. The figure is commonly referred to as the closing balance e.g. the total amount owed by customers is the debtors closing balance.

The closing balances are the balances at close of business, at a cut off point, e.g. the date of the Balance Sheet. All the closing balances make up the Balance Sheet.

So, for example:

Debtors

	£
Sales made during this year	58000
Less Payments made by customers in the year	53000
Balance owed by customers at the end of the year (closing Debtors)	5000

The £5,000 will appear on the Balance Sheet as the Debtors' closing balance (or just Debtors), an Asset.

As well as Debtors, using the information above, there is another Asset. Customers have paid £53,000 so there is money or cash. Cash is an Asset on the Balance Sheet. Let us say that the money has all been paid into the bank.

The Profit and Loss account on p17 showed sales of £58,000 AND total expenses of £33,000. Let us say those expenses have all been paid and have been paid out of the bank:

	£
Money in bank at beginning of the year	Nil
Plus Money paid in (from Customers)	53000
Total	53000
Less money paid out (Business Expenses – see P & L above – all paid, none owed)	33000
Bank balance at end or closing balance	20000

...cont'd

The bank, of course, summarise this for you on your bank statements.

Usually something like this:

Bank Statement	Out	In
	£	£
Money at beginning or opening balance		Nil
Sales paid		53000
Expenses paid -		
Materials Purchased	16000	
Wages	8000	
Premises	2500	
Repairs & Maintenance	500	
Motor	2000	
Office or Administration	1500	
Advertising	2000	
Accountancy	500	
Total Expenses paid	33000	
Bank balance at end or closing balance	20000	

Each figure is the total of many transactions appearing on the bank statement.

NOTE: The money in the bank is only £20,000 not £25,000 shown by the Profit and Loss account because £5,000 of the sales have not been paid.

The layout above is the way your bank statements tend to look with Money Out on the left and Money In on the right.

So the full Balance Sheet at the end of the year will look like this:

Balance Sheet		£
Assets		
Debtors (Sales not yet paid for)		5000
Cash at Bank		20000
Total Assets	A	25000
Liabilities		
Creditors (Expenses not yet paid for)		Nil
Total Liabilities	B	Nil
NET ASSETS	A – B	25000

However, the Balance Sheet is not complete with just Assets and Liabilities.

There is more information on the Balance Sheet than Assets & Liabilities. There is a **CAPITAL ACCOUNT.**

What is a Capital Account?

To understand the Capital Account, you have to think of the business as separate from the owner.

The business is like a separate person (and if the business is a Company, it is a separate person in law).

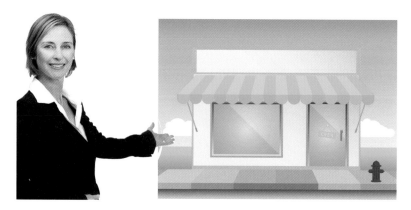

Owner   **Business**

The business is a new shop. It opens its doors on Monday with goods to sell. It has bought the goods from a supplier and owes the supplier for the goods.

At the end of Monday it has sold all the goods for cash and paid the supplier for the goods out of the money in the till.

It sold the goods for more than it paid for them and so has made a profit and that profit is the money sitting in the till.

The owner has set up and organised the business whether she has carried on the business herself or paid others to do it. The business has made a profit. The profit is owed to the owner. It is her business. That profit is hers.

If she doesn't take the Profit, it is recorded in the Capital Account. The Capital Account is her record of what is owed to her at the end of each year.

The Capital Account could look like this:

Capital Account	£
Profit of Year 1	25000
Less paid to owner (Drawings)	NIL
Undrawn (and carried forward to Year 2)	25000

(the Profit of £25,000 is the profit from our Profit & Loss on p17).

The Balance Sheet shows the Capital Account as above except the undrawn £25,000 will then be carried forward and shown as Capital Account Carried Forward (or CF).

Balance Sheet		£
Assets		
Debtors (Sales not yet paid for)		5000
Cash at Bank*		20000
Total Assets	A	**25000**
Liabilities		
Creditors (Expenses not yet paid for)		Nil
Total Liabilities	B	**Nil**
Net Assets	A–B	25000
Capital Account Brought Forward (BF)		Nil
Plus Profit		25000
Capital Account Carried Forward (CF)		**25000**

The Net Assets of £25,000 match the Capital Account CF £25,000.

...cont'd

If the business realised all its Assets (collected the £5,000 owed by its customers) and paid off all its Liabilities on the Balance Sheet date, the money sitting in the business bank account would be £25,000 matching what the business owed the owner.

After debts had been collected from Customers:

Balance Sheet	£
Assets	
Cash at Bank	25000
Liabilities	Nil
Net Assets	25000
Capital Account CF	25000

Note that the Net Assets still match the Capital Account.

A summary of the bank statement would be:

Bank Statement	Out £	In £
Money at beginning or opening balance		Nil
Sales paid		53000
Expenses paid -	33000	
Debtors paid		5000
Bank balance at end or closing balance	25000	

If the owner took the £25,000 out of the bank (known as Drawings), there would then be nothing in the bank and nothing owed to the owner. There would be nothing on the Balance Sheet:

Balance Sheet	£
Assets	
Cash at Bank	Nil
Liabilities	Nil
Net Assets	Nil
Profit	25000
Less Drawings	25000
Capital Account CF	Nil

Net Assets still match Capital Account CF, i.e. NIL.

We have shown you the owner taking all his money because this will help you understand the relationship between Net Assets and the Capital Account.

Balance Sheet so far...

- Customers who have not paid for the goods or services they have had are referred to as Debtors
- Suppliers that have not been paid are called Creditors
- The balance sheet is a snapshot of what the business is worth on one day
- The Balance Sheet shows Assets, Liabilities & Capital Account
- Assets are things of value belonging to the business e.g. property, equipment, debtors and stock
- Liabilities are things that the business owes e.g. creditors and loans

...cont'd

- Net Assets are Assets less Liabilities

- The owner and the business are separate and the business owes the owner what is in the Capital Account. The Capital Account is represented by the Net Assets. If the business sells the Assets and pays off the Liabilities what is left will equal the Capital Account and belongs to the owner

Now let's be sensible!

However, it would not be sensible for the owner to take all the Profit because the business would have no money left to buy anything it needed. So let us work on the basis that the owner did **not** take all the money but instead only took **some** money to live on.

So on the basis that the owner did not realise all Assets and pay off all Liabilities, going back to the Balance Sheet above, this is where we were:

Balance Sheet		£
Assets		
Debtors (Sales not yet paid for)		5000
Cash at Bank		20000
Total Assets	**A**	**25000**
Liabilities		
Creditors (Expenses not yet paid for)		Nil
Total Liabilities	**B**	**Nil**
Net Assets	A–B	25000
Capital Account Brought Forward (BF)		Nil
Plus Profit		25000
Capital Account Carried Forward (CF)		25000

To introduce more realism to our Balance Sheet, supposing instead of Nil Liabilities at the year end, let us say £2,000 was owed to Suppliers for goods or services purchased (in other words the business had Creditors):

Balance Sheet	£
Assets	
Debtors (Sales not yet paid for)	5000
Cash at Bank	22000*
Total Assets	**27000**
Liabilities	Nil
Creditors (Expenses not yet paid for)	2000
Total Liabilities	**2000**
Net Assets	25000
Capital Account BF	Nil
Plus Profit	25000
Capital Account Carried Forward (CF)	25000

* The cash at bank was £20,000 but we are now saying that £2,000 is owed to creditors, so £2,000 was not paid out of the bank to suppliers.

There is therefore £2,000 more in the bank – £20,000 plus £2,000 gives £22,000.

...cont'd

A summary of a bank statement would be:

Bank Statement		
	Out £	In £
Money at beginning or opening balance		Nil
Sales paid		53000
Expenses paid -		
Materials Purchased (£16000 less Suppliers not paid, £2000)	14000	
Wages	8000	
Premises	2500	
Repairs & Maintenance	500	
Motor	2000	
Office or Administration	1500	
Advertising	2000	
Accountancy	500	
Bank balance at end or closing balance	22000	

You can see how introducing something new, changes the accounts in **TWO** places by the same amount.

Suppliers being owed £2,000 introduces Creditors of £2,000 into the Balance Sheet AND the bank balance goes up £2,000 to £22,000 (£20,000 + £2,000). **Both** creditors **and** bank balance are changed by £2,000.

Let us say also that the owner took £18,000 of the Profit for himself (drawings), £1,500 every month throughout the year. This is another change that affects the bank balance.

The Balance Sheet would look like this:

Balance Sheet		£
Assets		
Debtors		5000
Cash at Bank		4000*
Total Assets	A	9000
Liabilities		
Creditors (Expenses not yet paid for)		2000
Total Liabilities	B	2000
Net Assets	A-B	7000
Capital Account BF		Nil
Plus Profit		25000
Less Drawings		18000
Capital Account Carried Forward (CF)		7000

*Cash at bank had been £22,000 but now the owner has taken £18,000 to live on the cash at bank is £4,000.

...cont'd

A bank statement might look like this:

Bank Statement

	Out £	In £
Money at beginning or opening balance		Nil
Sales paid		53000
Expenses paid -		
Materials Purchased (£16000 less Suppliers not paid, £2000)	14000	
Wages	8000	
Premises	2500	
Repairs & Maintenance	500	
Motor	2000	
Office or Administration	1500	
Advertising	2000	
Accountancy	500	
Drawings	18000	
Bank balance at end or closing balance	4000	

Again introducing something new, changes the accounts in **TWO** places by the same amount.

The owner taking £18,000 drawings affects the Capital Account on p33 which comes down to £7,000 (£25,000 - £18,000) AND the bank balance which comes down to £4,000 (£22,000 - £18,000). Both Capital Account and bank balance are changed by £18,000.

If the owner or proprietor of the business had put some of his own money into the business perhaps to help buy something expensive for the business like a vehicle because the business did not have the money at the time, this is commonly known as Capital Introduced and the Capital Account might look like this:

Capital Account	£
Capital Account BF	Nil
Plus Profit of Year	25000
Plus Money from Owner (Capital Introduced)	1000
Total	26000
Less Drawings	18000
Capital Account CF	8000

Within the Capital Account £8,000, is the £1,000 capital introduced.

Because everything is added together, i.e. Capital Account BF, Profit, Capital Introduced and Drawings and the end result is the Capital Account, it is not necessary in sole trader or partnership accounts to try to establish what relates to what, just what the end position is. That is at the end of the year, the business owes the owner £8,000.

...cont'd

Putting eveything together the balance sheet will look like this:

Balance Sheet		£
Assets		
Debtors		5000
Cash at Bank		5000*
Total Assets	A	10000
Liabilities		
Creditors		2000
Total Liabilities	B	2000
Net Assets	A-B	8000
Capital Account BF		Nil
Plus Profit		25000
Plus Capital Introduced		1000
Less Drawings		18000
Capital Account CF		8000

*The Capital Introduced was £1,000. The Cash at bank has gone up by the £1,000 from the owner.

And the bank statement like this:

Bank Statement

	Out	In
	£	£
Money at beginning or opening balance		Nil
Sales paid		53000
Expenses paid -		
Materials Purchased (£16000 less Suppliers not paid, £2000)	14000	
Wages	8000	
Premises	2500	
Repairs & Maintenance	500	
Motor	2000	
Office or Administration	1500	
Advertising	2000	
Accountancy	500	
Drawings	18000	
Capital Introduced		1000
Bank balance at end or closing balance	5000	

...cont'd

We said that the owner might need to lend the business some money to purchase something expensive like a vehicle. So let us say that this was the reason the owner lent the business £1,000 and the vehicle cost £4,000. Although the business had just enough money in the bank to buy the vehicle, the owner did not think it was a good idea to use a big chunk of the money that was in the business bank account, in case it left the business unable to pay future expenses.

After buying the vehicle the Balance Sheet might look like this:

Balance Sheet		£
Assets		
Vehicle		4000
Debtors (Sales not yet paid for)		5000
Cash at Bank		1000
Total Assets	A	**10000**
Liabilities		
Creditors		2000
Total Liabilities	B	**2000**
Net Assets	A-B	8000
Capital Account BF		Nil
Plus Profit		25000
Plus Capital Introduced		1000
Less Drawings		18000
Capital Account CF		8000

Again the Balance Sheet changes in 2 places - the business now owns a £4,000 vehicle AND the money in the bank has gone down by £4,000 (from £5,000 to £1,000).

And the bank statement like this:

Bank Statement

	Out	In
	£	**£**
Money at beginning or opening balance		Nil
Sales paid		53000
Expenses paid -		
Materials Purchased (£16000 less Suppliers not paid, £2000)	14000	
Wages	8000	
Premises	2500	
Repairs & Maintenance	500	
Motor	2000	
Office or Administration	1500	
Advertising	2000	
Accountancy	500	
Drawings	18000	
Capital Introduced		1000
Vehicle purchased	4000	
Bank balance at end or closing balance	1000	

The owner had to lend the business £1,000 so the business had a little money left after purchasing the vehicle. Remember there was only £4,000 in the bank account before the owner put in the £1,000 capital introduced.

...cont'd

If the owner did not have any money to put into the business, he could have gone to the bank and asked for a loan of £1,000 instead. Then if the bank had given the loan, the Balance Sheet would have looked like this:

Balance Sheet		£
Assets		
Vehicle		4000
Debtors		5000
Cash at Bank		1000
Total Assets	A	10000
Liabilities		
Creditors		2000
Bank Loan		1000
Total Liabilities	B	3000
Net Assets	A-B	7000
Capital Account BF		Nil
Plus Profit		25000
Less Drawings		18000
Capital Account CF		7000

The capital introduced disappears and is replaced by a Bank Loan under Liabilities.

And the bank statement like this:

Bank Statement

	Out £	In £
Money at beginning or opening balance		Nil
Sales paid		53000
Expenses paid -		
Materials Purchased (£16000 less Suppliers not paid, £2000)	14000	
Wages	8000	
Premises	2500	
Repairs & Maintenance	500	
Motor	2000	
Office or Administration	1500	
Advertising	2000	
Accountancy	500	
Drawings	18000	
Capital Introduced		0
Vehicle purchased	4000	
Bank Loan		**1000**
Bank balance at end or closing balance	1000	

Hot tip

Get your customers to pay promptly to avoid having to find money yourself to support the business when the bank balance gets low.

It is interesting to note that if the customers who owed money (i.e. the debtors of £5,000) had paid what was owed, no extra money would have been needed because there would have been another £5,000 in the bank account i.e. plenty of money!

...cont'd

We have shown you a summary bank statement for the year each time a change has been made. In reality of course there would be lots of transactions spread throughout the year and monthly statements.

The bank statement is one of the most important documents in accounts. The information is complete and can be relied upon. Invoices/bills may not be issued for every transaction (although of course they should be) and can be lost.

Accounts with a Balance Sheet have to include **ALL** the bank transactions or it will not be possible to match the bank balance shown on the Balance Sheet with the figure on the bank statement at the Balance Sheet date. The bank statement is the one solid piece of information from which accounts can be prepared.

A full set of Accounts comprises the Balance Sheet and the Profit & Loss so the Balance Sheet above and the Profit & Loss opposite.

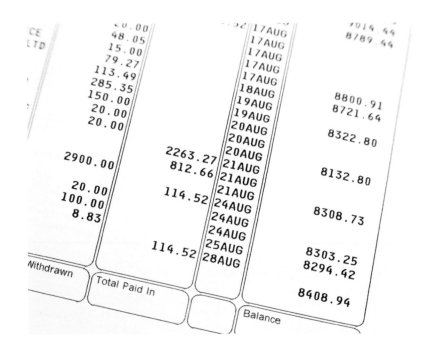

Here is the Profit and Loss account again:

Year Ended 31st March		
Profit & Loss Account	£	£
Sales (or Work Done)		**58000**
Less Expenses		
Materials Purchased	16000	
Wages	8000	
Premises	2500	
Repairs & Maintenance	500	
Motor	2000	
Office or Administration	1500	
Advertising	2000	
Accountancy	<u>500</u>	**33000**
Profit		**25000**

NOTE

The Profit & Loss did not change as we changed our examples above. The Profit remained at £25,000 and that was the figure of Profit in each of the Balance Sheets. This is because all the changes we made were to the Assets & Liabilities in the **Balance Sheet**, none were to the Sales and Expenses in the **Profit and Loss**.

Capital Accounts - Partnerships

Remember the Capital Account is what the business owes the owner. Here we have two owners.

In a Partnership, each owner (partner) has their own Capital Account.

Here is a Partnership Capital Account with two partners. There are two examples. In the first, the partners are 50/50 partners i.e. they share profits (or losses) equally.

In the second they are 75/25.

We have assumed that each partner has drawn £750 pm, £9,000 for the year:

Partners 50/50

	Partner A	Partner B	Total
	50%	50%	
	£	£	£
Capital Account BF	Nil	Nil	
Plus Profit of year	12500	12500	25000
Less Drawings	9000	9000	18000
Capital Account CF	3500	3500	7000

Partners 75/25

	Partner A	Partner B	Total
	75%	25%	
	£	£	£
Capital Account BF	Nil	Nil	
Plus Profit of year	18750	6250	25000
Less Drawings	9000	9000	18000
Capital Account CF	9750	-2750	7000

You can see that in the 72/25 partnership, Partner B's Capital Account has gone into minus i.e. instead of the business still owing him for profits it has made, he now owes the business because he has drawn out more than his share of the profits. In effect Partner A is supporting him.

Summary

- There can be lots of items on the Balance Sheet e.g. vehicles, debtors, creditors etc and each figure is the balance or total of all the transactions for each item

- The balances of every item are gathered together on the Balance Sheet

- The Balance Sheet is made up of two parts – Net Assets (Assets less Liabilities) and Capital Account

- The Capital Account is represented by the Net Assets of the business

- The Capital Account and Net Assets always match or a mistake has been made

- The Balance Sheet shows Assets, Liabilities and Capital Account, and the Profit & Loss shows Income and Expenses. The two complement each other and together give a complete picture

- The Profit & Loss shows the Income & Expenses of the business whether or not they have been paid. The Balance Sheet shows what is owed and the overall worth of the business

- The Balance Sheet and a Profit & Loss Account make up a full set of accounts

Now you have general understanding of accounts, what other records does a business need to keep to enable a full set of accounts to be prepared?

4 Record Keeping

Accounts are only as accurate as the records from which they are prepared

Records Required

Hot tip

Scan records and keep them electronically to save storage.

A business should keep a record of:

- All sales

- All purchases and other expenses

- All assets

- All liabilities

- Drawings

- All monies coming in and going out i.e. bank, cash and credit/debit cards payments

- Any goods unsold at the year end i.e. stock

From its records, a business should be able to identify what is owed to the business (debtors) and what the business owes (creditors).

Properly completed bank statements and legible cheque books and paying-in slips are essential. As internet banking takes over, it will be important to clearly describe internet transactions when making internet transfers or print out bank statements and make notes on them. The noted bank statements should be kept or scanned and saved as an electronic record.

It is very frustrating to look at a bank transaction which took place only weeks previously and not know what it is. If a business does not review its bank statements **regularly,** you may have no idea whatever what transactions are and will have to ask the bank for more information.

The Law

What records do I have to complete by law?

- Companies are required by law to keep accounting records whether or not they are trading

- By law, they must keep the records listed on p48

- They must be available for inspection by any of the company's officers (directors, company secretaries) at all times

- Under tax law, **all** businesses are expected to keep their records for basically the last **six tax years**

- Businesses need to keep extra records if they employ people – see p58

Beware

HMRC will challenge records that they suspect are fictitious or have been altered, for example, to inflate the purchase price of goods or to make a bill for something personal look like something for the business. This is obviously fraud and criminal and HMRC take a very serious view and will consider prosecuting people that do this.

What's the Minimum?

What are the minimum record books I must complete?

The Cashbook

"Cash" in accountancy terms is used to describe any transaction which is paid immediately, however paid, e.g. with cash or by cheque or debit card, as opposed to transactions which will be paid later i.e. are on credit.

The Cashbook can be a record of each transaction e.g. every invoice or bill and how it has been paid. HMRC will expect a Cashbook to be kept especially if the business is VAT registered.

In this book, we use the word "Invoices" when talking about Sales, and "Bills" when talking about Expenses.

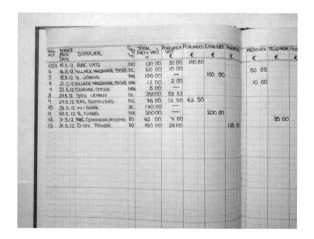

A completed paper Cashbook looks like this.

If you are not VAT registered then you will not use the 'VAT' column.

A completed computer Cashbook looks very similar.

There would probably be two spreadsheets, one for Income and one for Expenses.

This spreadsheet is Income or Sales:

Invoice Number	Invoice Date	Invoice Paid Date	How Paid	Customer	Total (Net + VAT)	Sales VAT	Sales

A completed Income spreadsheet might look like this if the business was **not** VAT registered:

Invoice Number	Invoice Date	Invoice Paid Date	How Paid	Customer	Total (Net + VAT)	Sales VAT	Sales
059	15/4/12	30/4/12	Bank	D Smith	1200.00		1200.00
060	16/4/12	16/4/12	Bank	J Singh	2400.00		2400.00
061	17/4/12	1/5/12	Bank	A Green	720.00		720.00
062	20/4/11	10/5/11	Bank	M Khan	4800.00		4800.00

It would look like this if the business **was** VAT registered:

Invoice Number	Invoice Date	Invoice Paid Date	How Paid	Customer	Total (Net + VAT)	Sales VAT	Sales
059	15/4/12	30/4/12	Bank	J Smith	1200.00	200.00	1000.00
060	16/4/12	16/4/12	Bank	J Singh	2400.00	400.00	2000.00
061	17/4/12	1/5/12	Bank	A Green	720.00	120.00	600.00
062	20/4/11	10/5/11	Bank	M Khan	4800.00	800.00	4000.00

The "Total (Net + VAT)" column comes before the "Sales VAT," and "Sales" columns because it helps you match the figure with other paperwork e.g. bank statements. The first entry £1,200 will be the figure on the bank statement.

This spreadsheet is Expenses. It would have many more Expenses categories than the four shown below (Purchases, Wages, Premises, Repairs & Maintenance) but these serve our purpose of illustrating:

Bill Ref	Invoice Date	Invoice paid Date	Cheque No	Supplier	Total (Net + VAT)	Purchase VAT	Net Expenses			
							Purchases	Wages	Premises	Repairs & Maintenance

Purchases are goods and materials purchased. Other expenses might be – telephone, insurance, motor, travel and subsistence (meals), advertising, accountancy etc.

People often do not know where to start with a Cashbook unless they have had accountancy or bookkeeping training.

They can EITHER enter all the invoices and bills OR all the bank & cash transactions. It is difficult to make the cashbook do both easily

It is advisable to ensure every invoice and bill has a reference number so the number can be entered in the Cashbook. You can write the number in the top right hand corner of the bill and number them consecutively.

It is advisable to file the bills in order you have numbered them. That way, you will be able to easily find the bill if a query arises at a later date.

Instead of entering every invoice and bill, you can record just bank and cash transactions and keep invoices together that are paid together.

E.g. if the business receives a supplier statement showing three invoices and pays the statement, find the invoices and pin them to the statement, and enter the transaction as one line in the Cashbook.

Let us assume that the business is not registered for VAT.

Let us say you have three invoices for goods purchased as follows:

Bill Ref	Date	Supplier	Description	£
1	12.4.12	ABC Ltd	Purchases	24.00
2	20.4.12	ABC Ltd	Purchases	48.00
3	1.5.12	ABC Ltd	Purchases	48.00

and you pay all three with a cheque number 010 for £120 on 15.5.12.

You can EITHER enter the invoices separately:

Bill Ref	Invoice Date	Invoice paid Date	Cheque No	Supplier	Total (Net + VAT)	Purchase VAT	Net Expenses			
							Purchases	Employee	Premises	Repairs & Maintenance
					£	£	£	£	£	£
1	12/4/12	15/5/12	010	ABC Ltd	24.00		24.00			
2	20/4/12	15/5/12	010	ABC Ltd	48.00		48.00			
3	1/5/12	15/5/12	010	ABC Ltd	48.00		48.00			

The three invoices are paid with the same cheque so the same "Invoice paid date" and "Cheque no" is entered beside each invoice

OR

just use one line for the payment (representing three invoices – 1, 2 & 3):

Bill Ref	Invoice Date	Invoice paid Date	Cheque No	Supplier	Total (Net + VAT)	Purchase VAT	Net Expenses			
							Purchases	Employee	Premises	Repairs & Maintenance
					£	£	£	£	£	£
1/2/3		15/5/12	010	ABC Ltd	120.00		120.00			

If the business was VAT registered, the Cashbook would look like this:

Bill Ref	Invoice Date	Invoice paid Date	Cheque No	Supplier	Total (Net + VAT)	Purchase VAT	Net Expenses			
							Purchases	Employee	Premises	Repairs & Maintenance
					£	£	£	£	£	£
1	12/4/12	15/5/12	010	ABC Ltd	24.00	4.00	20.00			
2	20/4/12	15/5/12	010	ABC Ltd	48.00	8.00	40.00			
3	1/5/12	15/5/12	010	ABC Ltd	48.00	8.00	40.00			

OR

like this if you use just one line:

Bill Ref	Invoice Date	Invoice paid Date	Cheque No	Supplier	Total (Net + VAT)	Purchase VAT	Net Expenses			
							Purchases	Employee	Premises	Repairs & Maintenance
					£	£	£	£	£	£
1/2/3		15/5/12	010	ABC Ltd	120.00	20.00	100.00			

This way the Cashbook then becomes a listing of all the bank transactions often working from the bank statements but looking at cheque books, bank paying-in books, invoices and bills for more information as necessary.

...cont'd

Bills paid in cash can then be added.

So a Cashbook for a variety of expenses might look like this:

Bill Ref	Invoice Date	Invoice paid Date	Cheque No	Supplier	Total (Net + VAT)	Purchase VAT	Net Expenses			
							Purchases	Employee	Premises	Repairs & Maintenance
					£	£	£	£	£	£
1/2/3		15/5/12	010	ABC Ltd	120.00	20.00	100.00			
4		16/5/12	DC	Village Hardware Store	60.00	10.00				50.00
5		18/5/12	Bank Transfer	S. Johns	100.00	-		100.00		
6		21/5/12	Cash	Village Hardware Store	12.00	2.00				10.00

DC = Debit Card

How to run a business with a cashbook and 4 folders

You can run a business with just a cashbook and 4 folders.

- 2 folders for sales invoices, one for paid and one for unpaid

- 2 folders for expenses invoices, paid and unpaid

As invoices are paid, note them how (e.g. cheque or cash) and when and just move them from the unpaid folder to the paid folder.

At the end of the year, list the unpaid sales invoices and these will be closing debtors. List unpaid expenses invoices and these will be your closing creditors.

Other Possible Record Books

- **SALES LEDGER** (Each customer is entered separately in the Sales Ledger together with each sales invoice to that customer and the payments the business has received from the customer)

- **PURCHASE LEDGER** (Each supplier is entered separately in the Purchase Ledger together with each purchase invoice from that supplier and the payments the business has made to the supplier)

- Possibly a **NOMINAL LEDGER** for all other business expenses, e.g. employee, office, motor, advertising, etc and everything else

- **WAGES BOOK** (only needed if you employ staff) – see below

- **SEPARATE PETTY CASH BOOK** where cash income and bills paid in cash are listed – see below

Remember it is a good idea to number each bill (e.g. in pencil, in the right hand corner) and advisable to file the bills in numerical order. You can note bill numbers in the records and be able to find the bill easily if a query arises at a later date.

If you number the bills when you are writing up the records. You will know that a bill with no number has not been entered into the records yet.

If you are not VAT registered then you have no need of the 'VAT' columns. VAT is covered in more detail later.

Don't forget

Whatever records you keep, you must update them regularly or you will forget what transactions were for.

Wages

The wages book

You will need to keep a record of how much you pay each employee and the deductions made from their wages.

For each employee you must keep a record of:

- Their gross pay (pay before tax)

- Any PAYE tax deducted or refunded

- Any National Insurance contributions (NICs) deducted

- Any Student Loan deductions

- Their net pay (pay after deductions)

You must give each employee a payslip with this information each time you pay them.

PAYE

PAYE is a method of calculating the tax and national insurance to be deducted from wages & salaries each time they are paid so that at the end of the tax year, the right amount of tax has been paid.

Employers have to deduct tax under PAYE by using a Code number.

HM Revenue & Customs (HMRC) provide a form - P11 Deductions Working Sheet - on which to manually record these details and keep as your wages records but it is much easier to use payroll software or pay a specialist payroll company to produce payslips for your employees and to file the necessary returns at the end of the year.

HMRC wish to move to a system where businesses have to inform them each week or month what employees have been paid. At present they only receive details of employee pay and tax/NIC deductions at the end of the tax year.

National minimum wage

Your employees must be paid the national Minimum Wage, an hourly rate which changes annually, usually in October. Your wages records will help you demonstrate that you are paying the national minimum wage (NMW). HMRC may carry out inspections of employers at any time. If you are found to have been paying less than the NMW, you will have to pay the difference, back-dated often at least six years together with the additional PAYE and National Insurance payable on the additional wages.

You will almost certainly also be fined and fines can be as much as 50% of the pay that you should have paid your employees. It is a criminal offence to deliberately pay less than the NMW, not to keep records for NMW and not to pay the NMW after HMRC have formally told you to. HMRC can use their search and seize powers under the Police and Criminal Evidence Act 1984 when investigating criminal offences under the National Minimum Wage Act 1998.

Beware

Flouting the National Minimum Wage can get you into serious trouble.

Petty Cash

Petty Cashbook

If the business receives cash or pays expenses in cash, it must keep adequate records.

HMRC would expect a Petty Cashbook to be kept showing cash received as well as cash spent and to be balanced weekly, i.e. cash received or "Cash In" for the week totalled and cash spent or "Cash Out" totalled and the balance compared to actual cash held.

Any difference should be noted and the Petty Cashbook figure adjusted accordingly:

	£	
Cash at start of week	50	A
Plus Business Cash received	100	B
Less Business Cash payments	20	C
Cash at end of week	130	(A+B-C)

Or represented another way:

	CASH IN	CASH OUT
	£	£
Cash at start of week	50	
Plus Cash received	100	
Less Cash payments		20
Cash at end of week		130
Total	150	150

Accountants always put Cash In on the left because this is in line with Double Entry bookkeeping, which is covered later in Chapter 8.

The business should count the money at the end of the week and compare it to what the records say it should be.

If it is different then you obviously need to try and find out why. Another entry should then be made in the Petty Cashbook to reconcile it to the actual cash held.

Say the actual money at the end of the week was £120 instead of £130 and you cannot find out what had happened to the missing £10, then you should make a note in the Petty Cashbook like this:

	£	
Cash at start of week	50	A
Plus Cash received	100	B
Less Cash payments	20	C
Cash at end of week	130	(A+B-C)
Less Missing Cash	10	
Actual Cash	120	

Or like this:

	CASH IN	CASH OUT
	£	£
Cash at start of week	50	
Plus Cash received	100	
Less Cash payments		20
Less missing Cash		10
Cash at end of week		120
Total	150	150

If you cannot find out why cash is missing, HMRC will assume that the owner has taken it, and the business may have to pay tax on it.

Hot tip

Recording and regularly reconciling the cash you should have with the cash you actually have, will ensure you identify problems such as staff pilfering early. It also shows you are in control of cash. Not recording cash may make HMRC suspicious that you are earning lots of cash that you are not declaring.

Hot tip

Many software packages have been created to assist businesses keep a full set of records. These are covered in little detail in Chapter 11.

Summary

- Business record books can consist of:

  – Cashbook

  – Sales Ledger

  – Purchase Ledger

  – Nominal Ledger

  – Wages Book

  – Petty Cashbook

- There is standard software available for this purpose. See Chapter 11

- The business must keep at least a Cashbook, either on paper or computer

- You must note invoices, bills and receipts, how and when they are paid to keep proper records and avoid getting in a muddle

- You can either record each invoice and bill and how it is paid OR record each payment and keep invoices/bills together that are paid together. You should number the bills

- If you do the former, the Cashbook is a record of every invoice and bill with information on payment. If you do the latter, the Cashbook is a record of bank and cash transactions with supporting invoices

- If you don't have any employees you can run a business with not much more than a Cashbook (computerised or manual) and 4 folders

5 Understanding Accounts

Annual Accounts

To get a better understanding of accounts let us look in detail at how they are put together.

The first question – what period do the accounts cover?

As already discussed, this is normally 12 months from the end of the last year's accounts or 12 months from the date the business started if a new business.

What should accounts consist of?

Accounts for a company must comply with the Company Act. Accounts for other businesses have no laid down format but would be expected to have a Profit & Loss (or Statement Of Income & Expenses) and preferably a Balance Sheet.

HMRC expect accounts to be drawn up in accordance with generally accepted accountancy rules and guidelines and may challenge any that are not.

Fundamental Accountancy Principles

Income and expenses matching and accruals

To arrive at accurate profit, it is important to identify all the sales for the period (say a year) and identify all the expenses that go to make those sales.

Sales may have been made but not invoiced by the end of the year. Expenses may have been paid in arrears (after the goods or services have been provided), or paid in advance (before the goods or services are provided).

An example of bills in arrears would be utility charges e.g. electricity, and for bills in advance, rent.

Bills in arrears

A bill received after the end of the year you are dealing with may include electricity used in that year. An estimate of the electricity used up to the year end needs to be included in the accounts as this electricity went directly or indirectly into making the sales of that year and should be reflected in the profit figure for that year.

E.g. The accounts being prepared are for the 12 months to 31st March. A bill for £600 is received from the electricity company dated 1st May for the electricity used in the 3 months to 30th April, i.e. for February, March and April.

The bill is dated after 31st March so would naturally be included in the following year's accounts because the date of the bill, 1st May, is after 31st March.

However some of the electricity was used in the year for which the accounts are being prepared. Some electricity needs to be included in that year. Accountants will split the bill and include part of it in one year and the other part in the following year.

In this case, they will include 2/3 of the bill (February & March) in the accounts for the year ended 31st March, so £400 (£600 x 2/3). 1/3 off the bill (April) will be included in the accounts for the following year so £200 (£600 x 1/3).

Bills in advance

Some of the bills might have to be taken out of the accounts if paid near the year end and it relates to the following year.

...cont'd

> *E.g. The accounts being prepared are for the 12 months to 31st March 2012. A bill for £2,500 was received for rent for the year beginning 1st October 2011, so from 1st October 2011 to the following 30th September 2012.*
>
> *October 2011 to March 2011 falls in our year and April to September 2012 (6 months) in the next year's accounts.*
>
> *£2,500 x 6/12 = £1,250 will be included in our accounts and £2,500 x 6/12 = £1,250 in the following year.*

So accounts must include all sales invoices and bills for expenses dated in the year, whether or not paid. They must also include sales that are made in the year and invoiced **after** it. They must also **include** expenses billed after the year end and must **exclude** expenses which relate to the following year.

In this way, expenses are matched with the sales they generate.

Accruals

Preparing accounts on this basis is commonly referred to as preparing accounts on an **accruals** basis.

There are various published accountancy standards or rules which accountants follow so that accounts are put together in the same way. We will come across one or two of these as we look at accounts.

Preparing accounts in a standardised way enables accounts to be interpreted more easily.

Earlier we looked at some very simple accounts. We are going to repeat some of the things we looked at then and also look at more items that you will see in everyday accounts.

> *Up to now, the layout of our "bank statements" has been the way most actual bank statements would look with "Money Out" on the left and "Money In" on the right. In Double Entry bookkeeping, it is the other way round.*

We are going to start to set out the examples in line with Double Entry bookkeeping to make it easier to understand Double Entry bookkeeping later. However, this book has been written to help you understand accounts without it being essential that you fully understand Double Entry bookkeeping.

Typical Profit & Loss Accounts

Let us look in detail at various items you would see in a typical Profit & Loss account.

Income (or Sales)

Income (or Sales) is the value of goods or services sold. We have seen that money for goods sold in a shop will almost certainly be described as Sales whereas the money earned by a builder who supplied materials and labour might be described "Work Done".

You may also hear the expression "Turnover". This is essentially the same as Sales but is used to describe the size of a business, e.g. a business with a high Turnover will be a business with high Sales and usually (but not always) a busy business with lots of transactions.

Credits/refunds

If goods bought in a shop are brought back perhaps because although not faulty, the customer does not like them or bought the wrong item, and the customer is refunded, the refund will probably be deducted from Sales. This reflects that first there was a sale and then this was reversed. Sales in the accounts will be shown after deducting refunds.

You will remember that we had Sales paid of £53,000 and Debtors of £5,000. Customers had not paid for £5,000 of the Sales. Let us say that actually sales were £58,500 and there were refunds of £500 giving net sales of £58,000. Then as before £5,000 of these sales had not yet been paid:

Sales	£
Sales Paid	53500
Plus Sales Owed (Debtors)	5000
Total Sales	58500
Less money refunded	500
Balance at end to be included in P & L	58000

...cont'd

The bank position will be as follows. In line with Double Entry bookkeeping we now need to put money In on the left and money Out on the right:

Bank Statement	In	Out
	£	£
Money at beginning or opening balance	Nil	
Sales paid	53500	
Sales refunds		500
Materials Purchased (£16000 less Suppliers not paid, £2000)		14000
Wages		8000
Premises		2500
Repairs & Maintenance		500
Motor		2000
Office or Administration		1500
Advertising		2000
Accountancy		500
Drawings		18000
Vehicle purchased		4000
Bank Loan	1000	
Bank balance at end or Closing Balance		1000

Business Expenses

Revenue & capital

Expenses fall into two categories:

1. **Revenue expenses** – these are the day-to-day expenses of the business, e.g. petrol for a business van

2. **Capital expenses** – these are the one-off expenses on something that will last for a while e.g. the van itself

Revenue expenses are included in the Profit and Loss. Capital expenses create an asset and will appear on the Balance Sheet.

Categorisation of revenue expenses

Revenue expenses include direct costs and indirect costs.

Direct costs

Direct costs are expenses that directly relate to producing or selling goods e.g. goods bought to sell in a shop (purchases) would be direct costs, as would the cost of the bags that the goods are put in when they are sold.

Raw materials purchased to manufacture a product would be direct costs as would the wages of staff working in the factory.

Commission paid to sales agents for the goods they sell for the business would be direct costs.

Direct costs increase or decrease as sales increase or decrease. E.g. the more goods a factory produces, the more raw material will be purchased. The more sales a shop makes, the more the shop will spend on purchases to replace the goods sold; the more bags it will need to use to carry the goods sold, etc.

If the costs do not result in the production of goods or the provision of services, and they do not vary with the volume of goods and services, they will probably not be direct costs.

A restaurant could be open with its lights on and staff standing ready and no-one come in for a meal. The cost of the electricity and the waiters' wages would be **indirect** costs. The business will spend money on electricity and staff whether or not the restaurant sells any meals i.e. has any sales.

...cont'd

If you identify direct costs, indirect costs or expenses will be anything else. They are commonly referred to as "Overheads". We will look at these later.

Purchases, stock and cost of goods sold

Stock is unsold or unused purchases i.e. goods and materials sitting on the shelves at the business premises waiting to be sold or used. A list of stock (a "stock take") needs to be made at the year end. Sometimes it is calculated from what is bought in less what has been sold but for small businesses the stock should usually be actually counted.

Goods purchased appear in the Profit and Loss as "purchases". But the figure of purchases in the P & L should be the purchases **that have been sold**. This is in line with the accountancy principles of matching expenses with the sales they relate to.

To work out the purchases that have been sold, start with the goods you had at the beginning of the year (so last year's stock if any) and add the cost of the goods purchased in the year. Together these are all the goods that the business had to sell. Take off the value of goods unsold at the year end (stock at year end) and what you have left is the value of goods that were actually sold in the year. This is referred to as the **Cost of Goods Sold** (or Cost of Sales).

Stock on hand at the beginning of the year is often referred to as Opening Stock. Stock at the end of the year, as Closing Stock.

So in Year 1 if you buy 16 items to use in your window installation business e.g. window units costing £1,000 each and during the year you sell 15 of them and have 1 unsold at the end of the year, then purchases in the accounts may look like this:

	£	
Purchases	16000	(16 x £1000)
Less closing stock	1000	(1 x £1000)
Cost of Goods Sold	15000	(15 x £1000)

The P & L will show the Cost of Goods Sold. Sometimes the P & L will show opening stock **and** purchases **and** closing stock to arrive at Cost of Goods Sold (COGS). Sometimes the P & L will just show the one figure of COGS. So, for Year 1 the P & L might show all 3 figures above or just COGS £15,000.

Let us look at the following year or Year 2.

So let us say that the business again bought 16 window units in Year 2 to sell and by the end of Year 2 had sold 15 of them and had 2 left, the position would be:

YEAR 2	£	
Opening Stock*	1000	(1 x £1000)
Plus Purchases	16000	(16 x £1000)
Total Purchases for resale	17000	(17 x £1000)
Less Closing Stock	2000	(2 x £1000)
Cost of Goods Sold (COGS)	15000	(15 x £1000)

*This is closing stock of Year 1

Work in Progress

Work in progress (WIP) is uncompleted work. You have paid out expenses to produce goods or services but they are not finished yet. The accountancy principle of matching expenses or costs with the income they generate applies to WIP.

So if you are say half way through a job at the end of your accounting year, then it might be logical to think that you should exclude from the accounts all the expenses relating to that job and put them in the following year when presumably the job will be invoiced to the Customer.

That is what used to happen. The expenses that related to unfinished work were calculated and WIP was deducted from expenses in the P & L much like Closing Stock and added in the following year as opening WIP.

However, then the accountancy bodies decided that instead of taking expenses **out** of the year and putting them in the following year, some of the sales for the following year should be brought **in** instead.

So say a job was half completed at the year end of Year 1, and when finished the customer was going to be invoiced £5000 in Year 2 (1 window unit £1000 plus profit on the job £4000). Under the new rules, half of the profit so £2000 would be included in the accounts for Year 1 even though the job was not finished and had not been invoiced yet.

As long as there is a reasonable expectation that the job will be finished and invoiced, then some of the profit on the job must be included in the year the job is started, based on how finished the job is at the year end.

So now the position in the accounts is in effect this:

YEAR 1	£
Sales	58000
Plus Work in progress (£4000 x 50%)	2000
Total Sales	60000

Or using another method of representing this:

YEAR 1	£	£
Sales		58000
Plus work in progress (£4000 x 50%)		2000
Balance at end for P & L	60000	
Total	60000	60000

So sales for Year 1 would be £2,000 higher because of the profit on the work in progress.

Note: The £1,000 window unit is still on the business' premises at the year end. It will be included in the accounts by being included in closing stock.

In Year 2 the job was finished and invoiced and let us pretend that no other jobs were done:

YEAR 2	£
Sales (window unit £1000 + profit £4000)	5000
Less opening work in progress (£4000 x 50%)	2000
Included in sales of Year 2	3000

Year 1's **closing** stock and WIP is Year 2's **opening** stock and WIP.

So you can see that in Year 2 when the job is invoiced for £5,000 (window unit £1,000 and profit £4,000), only half of the profit of £4,000 ends up as sales for Year 2, as half has already been included in sales in the previous year.

Gross Profit

Gross Profit is the profit after deducting Direct Costs, i.e. after Cost of Goods Sold. It is the profit before all the other expenses e.g. wages, premises, repairs, etc.

Buying something at £10 and selling it for £15 gives a Gross Profit of £5 (£15 - £10):

	£
Sales	15
Less Purchases	10
Gross Profit	5

Our Profit & Loss currently looks like this:

Year Ended 31st Mar		
Profit & Loss Account	£	£
Sales		60000
Less Expenses		
Cost of Goods Sold	15000	
Wages	8000	
Premises	2500	
Repairs & Maintenance	500	
Motor	2000	
Office or Administration	1500	
Advertising	2000	
Accountancy	500	32000
Profit		**28000**

Note that there are no new bank transactions. This is because the adjustments we have made for Stock and WIP do not involve money changing hands. The adjustments result in value (but not money) being moved around between accounts for different years so accounts are prepared on the accruals basis.

Using our Profit & Loss:

	£	£	
Sales		60000	A
Opening Stock	Nil		
Plus Purchases	16000		
Total	16000		
less Closing Stock	1000	15000	
Gross Profit		45000	B
Gross Profit Ratio/Percentage (B÷A x 100)		75%	

30% 40%
60% 10% 80%
50% 70% 20%
100% 90%

...cont'd

The full Profit & Loss will now look like this:

	£	£	
Sales		60000	
Opening Stock	Nil		
Plus Purchases	16000		
Total	16000		
less Closing Stock	1000	15000	
Gross Profit		45000	GPR 75%
Less Overheads			
Wages	8000		
Premises	2500		
Repairs & Maintenance	500		
Motor	2000		
Office or Administration	1500		
Advertising	2000		
Accountancy	500	17000	
Profit		**28000**	

If a business has had a GPR of 75% consistently year after year and this then drops to say 65% in the latest accounts prepared, there could be a variety of reasons or a combination of them.

It might be that the costs have gone up but the business has not been able to pass these on to customers by putting up prices because it fears it would drive customers away. The business has kept its prices the same and is prepared to make less profit rather than lose customers. So purchases have increased but not sales, leading to a drop in profit and therefore a drop in GPR.

It might be that competitors have started similar businesses nearby that are cheaper and the business that was there first has had to reduce its prices to stop customers switching to one of the other businesses. A drop in prices is a drop in sales and therefore profit and Gross Profit. So the reason here for a drop in GPR is that purchases remain similar but sales have reduced.

A drop in GPR could mean that shoplifting or staff pilferage has increased and goods are being stolen rather than being sold. Again a drop in sales affecting GPR.

So there could be a number of reasons for a marked change in GPR and a change in GPR is something to be concerned about until you can discover the likely reason.

Indirect Costs

Indirect Costs or Expenses (or overheads) are money spent on:

- Employees' Salaries & Wages

- Business premises, including rent, business rates, utility bills (electricity, gas, water)

- Repairs and maintenance of premises and equipment

- Administration costs such as stationery, postage, telephone and fax and computer software with a limited life

- Insurance

- Advertising & Marketing, Website maintenance

- Motor Vehicle expenses

- Staff Travel & Meals (Subsistence) while on business

- Professional Services e.g. accountants, solicitors

- Finance Interest & Charges, e.g. bank overdraft interest and bank charges

- Miscellaneous Costs such as trade or professional journals or subscriptions

- Bad debts (debts owed by customers that the business believes will never be paid and has written off)

Employees have to have tax and national insurance deducted from their wages/salaries under PAYE. Expenses for employees will include the pay the staff receive and all payments of PAYE tax & national insurance.

Bad debts

If some of the goods the business has sold on credit (i.e. Sales) are not going to be paid for perhaps because the customer has disappeared and cannot be traced, then the business is entitled to write off the debt and claim it as an expense in the P & L.

Let us say £350 of the amount owed by debtors will not be paid.

This is how the accounts will look. So you can see this easily we have shown **only** the sales and the bad debt, and no other expenses:

Simple Profit & Loss Account Year Ended 31st March

		£
Sales (or Work Done)		350
Less **Expenses**		
Materials Purchased		
Premises		
Motor		
Office or Administration		
Advertising		
Accountancy		
Bad Debts	350	350
Profit		0

Balance Sheet

Assets		£
Debtors		0
(Debtors £350 less Bad Debt £350)		
Total Assets	A	0
Liabilities		
Total Liabilities	B	0
Net Assets	A – B	0
Capital Account BF		
Plus Profit		0
Less Drawings		0
Capital Account CF		0

Depreciation

Depreciation is an allowance for vehicles, equipment or fixtures and fittings wearing out. It is included in the accounts as an expense like wages or premises.

> *Fixtures & Fittings – these are items that are attached firmly or loosely to premises e.g. central heating boilers and radiators, basins, toilets, furniture, carpets, etc.*

Depreciation is often 25%. It may be calculated using one of two methods:

1 On a reducing balance basis

2 On a straight line basis

Reducing Balance basis

Let us say a vehicle was purchased for £4000:

Year in which vehicle bought	£
Cost of vehicle	4000.00
less Depreciation 25%	1000.00
Value at year end (written down value)	3000.00

> *NB It does not matter when in the year the vehicle is bought e.g. it could be bought on the last day of the year, it would still normally be depreciated by 25%.*

The depreciation of £1,000 would be an expense in the P & L. Then the following year, depreciation is 25% of the written down value so

Following Year	£
Value at beginning of year	3000.00
less Depreciation 25%	750.00
Value at year end (written down value)	2250.00

The depreciation of £750 would be an expense in the following year's P & L.

This method is calculating depreciation on a reducing balance basis.

Straight Line basis

The life of the asset is estimated and the same depreciation claimed as an expense every year. So if you expect a vehicle costing £4,000 to last 10 years before it was scrap (Nil value), depreciation of £400 would be claimed each and every year for 10 years:

Year in which vehicle bought	£
Cost of Vehicle	4000
less depreciation	400
Written down value (WDV) at the end of Year 1	3600

At the end of the 10 years the position would be:

	£
Cost of Vehicle	4000
Less Depreciation £400 pa x 10 yrs	4000
Written down value (WDV) at the end of Year 10	Nil

Because electronic equipment like computers becomes obsolete after only a few years, a business might decide to depreciate the equipment over just 4 years so if the £4,000 above was not a vehicle but computers, the depreciation claimed each year might be £1,000.

At the end of the 4 years, electronic equipment will be wriiten down to NIL:

	£
Cost of Equipment	4000
Less Depreciation £1000 pa x 4 yrs	4000
Written down value (WDV) at the end of Year 4	Nil

Don't forget

Depreciation is not an actual money transaction i.e. it is not an expense that is actually paid. It is an estimate of the amount vehicles/ equipment have worn or devalued in the year of the accounts.

However, depreciation is most often calculated on a reducing balance. It takes 25 years to arrive at a value of Nil (or almost Nil) for vehicle or equipment when depreciation is 25% and is calculated on a reducing balance.

The figure for depreciation in the Profit & Loss is the total of the depreciation on the various different assets e.g. Vehicles, Equipment, Fixtures & Fittings, etc.

Depreciation is normally shown at the end of all expenses in the
Profit & Loss:

	£	£
Sales		60000
Opening Stock	Nil	
Plus Purchases	16000	
Total	16000	
less Closing Stock	1000	15000
Gross Profit		45000 GPR 75%
Less Overheads		
Wages	8000	
Premises	2500	
Repairs & Maintenance	500	
Motor	2000	
Office or Administration	1500	
Advertising	2000	
Accountancy	500	
Bad Debt	350	
Depreciation	1000	18350
Profit		26650

...cont'd

Once again, the bank transactions have not changed, as depreciation does not involve money changing hands. It is not actual money.

Selling the vehicle or equipment

Let us say that you sell the vehicle or equipment in the following year and you receive £3,000 then the position will be:

Following year	£
WDV* at beginning of year (from end of year 1)	3000.00
Sold (disposal)	3000.00
Profit/Loss on disposal	Nil

WDV – Written Down Value

After allowing for depreciation, the vehicle or equipment's written down value was £3,000 i.e. its estimated value prior to sale was £3,000, and it was sold for £3,000.

The business did not make either a profit or a loss on its sale.

The business will put the £3,000 received for the old one towards a new one.

Of course, it is very unusual for vehicles/equipment to be sold for exactly their Written Down Value.

Profit/loss on disposal

A loss is made when vehicles or equipment are sold for less than their value in the accounts.

So if in the following year, the vehicle bought for £4,000 was sold for £2,800 (rather then £3,000), the position would be:

Following Year	£
Value at beginning of year (WDV)	3000
Less Disposal	2800
Loss on Disposal	200

The Loss on Disposal is just like another expense, e.g. wages or premises. It appears in the P & L as "Profit/Loss on Disposal".

If you make a profit on the disposal of vehicles or equipment, the figure in the P & L for "Profit/Loss on Disposal" appears in brackets as a minus.

Say, the equipment had been sold for £3,100:

Following year	£
Value at beginning of year (WDV)	3000
Less Disposal	3100
Loss on Disposal	-100

Remember the business has included estimated depreciation in previous years' accounts as an expense. The Profit on Disposal merely claws back depreciation, which has been previously claimed so that the depreciation in the accounts agrees with the actual depreciation of the vehicle or equipment:

Year equipment bought	£
Cost	4000.00
less 25%	1000.00
Value at year end (WDV CF*)	3000.00

Following year	£
Value at beginning of year (WDV BF*)	3000.00
Disposal	3100.00
Loss on Disposal	-100.00

WDV CF – Written Down Value Carried Forward

WDV BF – Written Down Value Brought Forward

...cont'd

This is the overall position for the two years:

Total Depreciation allowed in the accounts	£
Depreciation in year equipment bought	1000
Loss on Disposal in year sold	-100
Overall depreciation in accounts	900

Actual depreciation on vehicle	£
Cost	4000
Less Disposal	3100
Actual depreciation	900

The Depreciation included in the P & L over the 2 years and Profit/Loss On Disposal equal the amount the vehicle actually depreciated.

Net Profit

Net Profit is the figure of profit after all expenses have been deducted (as opposed to Gross Profit which is after Direct Costs **only**). So the figure of £26,650 on p83 is more accurately described as "Net Profit £26,650".

Net profit before tax

Sole trader or partnership accounts **do not** show tax due on the business profits. This is because the tax is payable by the owner or partners, i.e. the individuals.

Company accounts **do** show the tax due because the tax is payable by the Company (as opposed to the owners or shareholders). This is what you will see in company accounts:

	£
Profit/Loss on ordinary activities before taxation (say)	31000
Less Tax on profit on ordinary activities (say 20%)	6200
Profit/Loss for the financial year (after tax)	24800

Other Profit & Loss Items

Insurance recoveries & grants

Insurance Recoveries and grants will commonly be included in the accounts under the category they relate to.

Insurance recoveries

An insurance claim for flooding of business premises, for example, will inevitably be made up of various components:

- Clearing up costs

- Replacement of equipment, carpets etc

- Compensation for lost profits i.e. lost sales while the damage was being sorted out

Say, the clearing up costs were £500 but the insurance company paid the business £400 for these. Then the clear up costs would probably be included in the accounts under repairs and the position would be as follows:

Repairs	£
Clear up costs	500
Less money refunded (Insurance Recovery)	400
Total and balance at end of year and claimed in Profit & Loss	100

Or as follows:

Repairs	£	£
Clear Up Costs	500	
Less money refunded (Insurance Recovery)		400
Balance at end and claimed in P & L		100
Total	500	500

So only £100 would appear in Repairs in the P & L, which is of course correct because the business did not end up actually paying the full costs. Of the total £500, the insurance company effectively paid £400 and the business paid £100.

If £4,000 of the money received from the insurance company was for loss of profits (sales), then the full position on Sales would be as follows:

Sales	£
Sales banked	53500
Less Sales refunds	500
Net Sales	53000
Plus owed (debtors)	5000
Plus Insurance Recovery banked	4000
Plus WIP	2000
Total Sales	64000

OR put another way:

Sales		
Description	£	£
Bank		53500
Bank (Sales Refunds)	500	
Owed (Debtors)		5000
Bank (Insurance Recovery)		4000
WIP		2000
Balance	64000	
Total	64500	64500

The £4,000 insurance recovery is for sales which the business would have had if it had not been flooded and for which the insurance company has paid instead.

Grants

A grant is normally given **for** something, often to help pay certain business expenses because an organisation wants to encourage or subsidise the business, and will be subject to certain conditions. A government may give a grant to a business to take on apprentices and help towards paying their wages.

In that case the position would be:

Wages	£
Money spent on Wages	8000
Less Grant received and paid into the bank	1000
Balance at end of year and claimed in P & L	7000

Or shown as below:

Wages	£	£
Wages	8000	
Less Grant		1000
Balance at end and claimed in P & L		7000
Total	8000	8000

The bank position taking into account the last few transactions would be as on the next page.

> Remember that in line with Double Entry bookkeeping, we are now putting money In on the left and money Out on the right which is probably the opposite of how they appear on bank statements.

Bank Statement	In	Out
	£	£
Money at beginning or opening balance	Nil	
Sales - Insurance recovery	4000	
Sales - from Customers	53500	
Sales refunds		500
Materials Purchased (£16000 less Suppliers not paid, £2000)		14000
Wages		8000
Grant - Wages	1000	
Premises		2500
Repairs & Maintenance		1900
Repairs (Insurance Recovery)	400	
Motor		2000
Office or Administration		1500
Advertising		2000
Accountancy		500
Drawings		18000
Vehicle purchased		4000
Bank Loan	1000	
Bank balance at end or closing balance		5000

Included in Repairs and Maintenance is £1,900 are the clear up costs following the flood of £500.

Profit and Loss in a nutshell...

So we have looked at the P & L in detail and have seen that:

- Sales and Work Done and Turnover are essentially the same, and that sales credits and refunds are commonly deducted from sales

- Business expenses can be capital or revenue. Revenue expenses appear in the P & L, capital expenses in the Balance Sheet

- Direct costs and purchases are the same and are directly linked to sales

- Direct costs/purchases are shown in the P & L as purchases sold or Cost of Goods Sold (COGS) after taking account of Stock (unused goods & materials) and Work in Progress (unfinished work)

- Gross Profit is sales less Cost of Goods sold (COGS) and is expressed as a percentage (GPR)

- Net Profit is Gross Profit less indirect costs and overheads such as wages, premises, repairs, etc including bad debts and depreciation (wear) on vehicles and equipment

- Tax is shown in company accounts (but not in the accounts of sole traders/partnerships) and is deducted from Net Profit

- Insurance recoveries and grants are added or deducted from the items they relate to e.g. insurance recovery for repairs is deducted from repairs

Typical Balance Sheet

Now we have looked at typical P & L items, we can turn to the Balance Sheet (BS). Some items appear in both P & L and BS e.g. Bad Debts (see p79).

Remember the Balance Sheet is made up of Assets and Liabilities, and Capital Account.

Assets can be Fixed or Current.

Fixed Assets

Fixed Assets can be:

- Fixed and tangible
- Fixed and intangible

Tangible Fixed Assets
Tangible fixed assets are property, vehicles, equipment, fixtures & fittings.

Assets can be shown in the Balance Sheet at their reduced value:

Year in which vehicle bought	£
Cost	4000.00
less Depreciation 25%	1000.00
Value at year end (written down value)	3000.00

NB: The depreciation of £1,000 also appears in the P & L.

Following year	£
Value at beginning of year	3000.00
less Depreciation 25%	750.00
Value at year end (written down value)	2250.00

So in the year the van is bought it appears in the BS at its cost of £4,000 but in the second year at its written down value of £3,000.

Remember though that we looked at what would happen if instead of being kept in the following year, the vehicle was sold that year for £2,800.

The vehicle would then be shown in the Balance Sheet as follows:

Following year	£
Value at beginning of year (WDV)	3000
Less Disposal	3000
Value at end of year	Nil

The vehicle is shown as being disposed of for its written down value **not what it was sold for**. This clears it out of the Balance Sheet because the business no longer owns it.

£2,800 was actually received. The van was valued at £3,000 in the BS so a loss of £200 was made on its disposal (£3,000 value less £2,800 received).

The £2,800 goes into the bank and the £200 goes to the P & L as a Loss on Disposal.

This example is just to show you what happens in the BS when a vehicle or equipment is sold.

However, in our accounts the van was not sold but was retained in the following year.

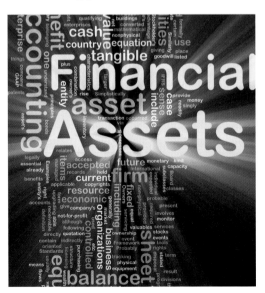

As an alternative to assets appearing in the BS at their written down value, assets can be shown at their original cost with depreciation shown separately. Both the depreciation that has been allowed in the past and the depreciation for the year are shown on the next page.

Year in which vehicle bought		£	
Cost	At 1 April 2012:	-	
	Plus Additions:	4000	
	Less Disposals:	-	
	At 31Mar 2013:	4000	A
Depreciation	At 1 April 2012:	-	
	Plus Charge for year:	1,000	
	On disposals:	–	
	At 31 Mar 2013:	1,000	B
Net book value	At 1 April 2012:	-	
	At 31 Mar 2013:	3000	A-B

The cost, depreciation and net book value are all shown separately:

Following year			
		£	
Cost	At 1 April 2013:	4000	
	Plus Additions:	-	
	Less Disposals:	-	
	At 31Mar 2014:	4000	A
Depreciation	At 1 April 2013:	1,000	
	Plus Charge for year:	750	
	On disposals:	–	
	At 31Mar 2014:	1750	B
Net book value	At 1 April 2013:	3000	
	At 31Mar 2014:	2250	A-B

...cont'd

Notice that the cost of the vehicle does not change, just the depreciation.

While the business still has the vehicle it always appears in the accounts at cost.

Again if instead of being kept in the following year, the vehicle had been sold for £2,800, the position would have been:

Following year		£	
Cost	At 1 April 2013:	4000	
	Plus Additions:	–	
	Less Disposals:	4000	
	At 31Mar 2014:	–	A
Depreciation	At 1 April 2013:	1,000	
	Plus Charge for year:	–	
	On disposals:	1000	
	At 31Mar 2014:	–	B
Net book value	At 1 April 2013:	3000	
	At 31Mar 2014:	–	A-B

The disposal value used for the vehicle is its cost £4,000 (not £2,800). The depreciation on disposal is the total depreciation that has been claimed £1,000.

Using these the vehicle is cleared out of the BS and the Net Book Value at 31st March 2014 is Nil.

Whether an asset is shown in the BS at its written down value or at cost, when it is disposed of, all trace of it is removed from the BS, as one would expect.

Intangible Fixed Assets

Intangible assets are defined by one of the accountancy bodies Standards (Financial Reporting Standard 10) as 'non financial fixed assets that do not have physical substance but are identifiable and are controlled by the entity (the business) through custody or legal rights'.

In other words they are not assets that you can see like property or vehicles but they have a value.

The best example of intangible assets is perhaps Goodwill.

What is Goodwill?

The Goodwill of a business is the good reputation of a business that leads to repeat business; and is part of the value of a business over and above the value of its premises, equipment, stock, etc.

Goodwill does not normally appear in the BS but will be calculated when the business is sold.

Goodwill can be zero at a point in time, e.g. an outbreak of food poisoning traced back to a restaurant can so damage the restaurant's trade that no-one wants to eat there.

Intangible assets can be depreciated. Although with goodwill a business would hope that it was increasing in value i.e. appreciating.

Current Assets

Current assets are assets that are fairly easily changed into money or realised.

Cash on hand and in the bank

These assets are the most current of all of course, because they are already money.

Debtors

Debtors are usually trade debtors, i.e. owed by customers or clients but there might be Other Debtors.

Other Debtors might be loans owed to the business by staff.

Debtors are still current assets because unless they are bad debts, they can be turned into money fairly quickly. Even if payment terms with customers are 30 days i.e. customers get 30 days from the date of the invoice before they have to pay, the debts will soon be money.

They appear in two places in the accounts:

1. Sales in the P & L (they are unpaid sales)

2. Debtors in the Balance Sheet (the customer owes the business for the sales)

Stock

Stock is unsold goods at the BS date. Stock is a current asset because it can be sold to produce money. A list of stock at the balance sheet date should have been made and totalled. The list should show the cost of each item.

If the item is no longer worth what was paid for it perhaps because it is unfashionable or obsolete, then it is acceptable to include it in the stock list at its lower resale or market value. The total of the list is the value of the stock and is included in the accounts.

Investments

Investments will be shown separately in the BS. Investments could be Stocks & Shares or perhaps a special bank account where money is invested for some time (money in a deposit account will often be included in cash on hand and in bank).

Liabilities

Creditors - short and long term

Short-term creditors are usually:

1. Trade creditors i.e. money owed to suppliers

2. HMRC e.g. VAT and/or PAYE that a business must deduct from its employees' wages and pay to HMRC

A loan repayable over several years would be a Long Term Creditor.

We have already looked at capital accounts above but here is a reminder on the next page.

Capital Accounts

The Capital Account will be made up of:

1. **Profit brought forward** – this is the profit from previous years that the owner has not spent

2. Plus **Profit of the year** – this is self explanatory

3. Plus **Capital Introduced** – this is money that the owner has lent the business from his own resources e.g. savings

4. Less **Drawings** – this is money taken or drawn from the business by the owner either profit that the business has made for him or perhaps money that he lent the business previously that he wants back

5. **Profit carried forward** (or Reserves) – this is the profit from previous years plus profit of the latest year that the owner has not spent

As you have seen in Chapter 3, separate capital accounts will be needed for each partner in a partnership.

The capital account in a limited company is usually known as Reserves/Retained Profits.

In addition to the Reserves/Retained Profits in a company, shareholdings appear on the Balance Sheet.

Balance Sheet in a nutshell...

- The BS shows Assets – Fixed and Current

- Fixed Assets can be intangible (like goodwill) or tangible (like property, vehicles, equipment, etc, after depreciation, or with depreciation shown separately

- Current Assets are trade debtors, stock, cash, money in the bank, and possibly short term investments

- The BS shows Liabilities – current (trade creditors and HMRC) and long term (loans)

- Assets less Liabilities give Net Assets

- The Capital Account matches Net Assets

- Remember many items appear in **both** P & L and BS

Accounts Fiddly Bits

It is useful for you to understand the changes or adjustments your accountant might make. We will call these "Accounts Fiddly Bits".

Accruals, provisions & prepayments
Accruals

You now know that accounts have to include costs that have been incurred but not yet billed e.g. electricity, and that an estimate is made of the costs and included in the accounts. This is called an accrual.

Accruals appear in two places:

1 In expenses in the P & L that they relate to e.g. Premises for electricity, and

2 In the Balance Sheet as Creditors & Accruals

This is because until the bill arrives and is paid, the expenses are owed just like any other unpaid transaction.

The example we have already used is an electricity bill for £600 which arrives the following year but covers some of the year we are dealing with.

It is worth going over the example again before we see how an Accrual appears in the accounts.

The accounts we are preparing are for the 12 months to 31st March. The electricity bill is dated 1st May and is for the electricity used in the quarter to 30th April, i.e. for February, March & April.

The bill is dated after the end of the 12 months to 31st March so would naturally be included in the following year's accounts because the date of the bill, 1st May, is after 31st March.

Because some of the electricity was used in our year, we need to include that in our financial year.

The bill covers three months: February, March & April. Two of the months, February & March are in our financial year. We must include 2/3 of the bill (2 months out of the 3 months), so £400 (£600 x 2/3).

We do this by adding £400 to premises in the P & L and putting an Accrual of £400 in the Balance Sheet as a Creditor (the electricity has not been paid in our year – it has not even been billed in our year!)

Premises	Year Ended 31st Mar	
	£	£
Electricity 1 Feb to 31st Mar (2 months)	400	
Balance at end and claimed in P & L		400
Total	400	400

The effect on the P & L will be to add more expenses. (For the purpose of illustrating this point we have not shown all the other expenses).

Year Ended 31st March (Year 1)		
Simple Profit & Loss Account		£
Sales (or Work Done)		-
Less Expenses		
Materials Purchased	-	
Premises (electricity)	400	
Motor	-	
Office or Administration	-	
Advertising	-	
Accountancy	-	
Profit/Loss on Disposal	-	400
Profit		-400

So with nothing else in the P & L, the electricity expense creates a **loss.**

...cont'd

The £400 appears in the BS as an additional liability and is matched by the extra expense in the P & L:

Balance Sheet		£
Assets		
Total Assets	**A**	**NIL**
Liabilities		
Accruals (electricity)		400
Total Liabilities	**B**	**400**
Net Assets	A – B	-400
Capital Account BF		NIL
Plus Profit		-400
Less Drawings		NIL
Capital Account CF		-400

There is a more common example of an accrual – accountancy fees. The cost of preparing the accounts is an expense of the business and needs to be included in the accounts that are being prepared despite the fact that the accountant is preparing the accounts some time after the end of the year.

We already have £500 worth of accountancy fees in the P & L which have been paid but we will assume that these were for helping with the payroll or for general business advice.

Let us say that the fees for preparing the accounts are £600 and just like the electricity accrual, we will include these fees (which will be billed after the year we are dealing with) as an Accrual in the BS.

So the P & L will show the accountancy fees paid of £500 plus the accountancy fees accrued of £600, total £1,100.

Again for clarity we have only shown the expenses that we have been dealing with not all the other expenses:

Year Ended 31st March (Year 1)		
Simple Profit & Loss Account		£
Sales (or Work Done)		–
Less <u>Expenses</u>		
Materials Purchased	–	
Premises	400	
Motor	–	
Office or Administration	–	
Advertising	–	
▶ Accountancy	1100	
Profit/Loss on Disposal		1500
Profit		-1500

The accountancy charges are £500 already paid plus £600 accrual:

Balance Sheet		
<u>Assets</u>		£
Total Assets	A	-
<u>Liabilities</u>		
▶ Accruals		1000[1]
Overdraft		-500[2]
Total Liabilities	B	1500
Net Assets	A – B	-1500
Capital Account BF		
Plus Profit		-1500
Less Drawings		
Capital Account CF		-1500

1. *Premises (Electricity) £400 + Accountancy £600 = £1,000*

2. *Note that there is an overdraft of £500 for the £500 already paid for accountancy fees and it is a liability.*

The other accruals of £400 for electricity and £600 for accountancy have not been paid (or even billed in our year). They have been "imported" into our accounts as they relate to the year we are dealing with.

...cont'd

Provisions

The business might feel that it has a liability or loss that is not shown in the accounts because it has not yet had a bill but perhaps expects to get one.

Let us say the business is in dispute about an accident it had during the year covered by the accounts. While the owner does not think he was to blame, he feels that he is likely to lose the dispute and have to pay some money to the other party, perhaps for some repairs. We will say that he thinks he will have to pay £800.

It would be normal for the accountant to estimate compensation that might be paid and include it the accounts.

He would claim the compensation as:

1   An expense in the P & L under the appropriate category and

2   Put a Provision in the BS just like for an Accrual

Prepayments

Once again it is worth reminding ourselves of the example.

The business paid a bill for storage rent for the 12 months beginning 1st October and the accounts year end is 31st March. Half of the bill relates to the year to 31st March (October to March), the last 6 months of the year. Half relates to the following year (April to September) the first 6 months of the following accounts year. So half the bill is deducted from the premises expenses and treated as a debtor. This is because half the expenses do not belong to the year you are dealing with but have all been paid in that year. Some have been paid on account of the following year and are owed to the business until included in the accounts for the following year.

£2,500 x 6/12 = £1,250 will be included in our accounts and £2,500 x 6/12 = £1,250 in the following year.

It might help you to think of it this way. If a business paid its rent as above but gave up the premises on 31st March, half of the rent that had been paid might be refunded.

So a Prepayment is in effect **deducted** from expenses and included in the BS as a Debtor. It is the opposite to an accrual which is added to expenses and included in the BS as a Creditor:

	£
Business rates 1 April to following 31st Mar (12 months)	2500
Less rates for period 1st Oct to following 31st Mar (6 months)	1250
Total and Balance at end of year and claimed in P & L	1250

The P & L will show the Premises (Rent) balance above, i.e. £1,250. To demonstrate once again we have only shown the item we are dealing with.

...cont'd

Year Ended 31st March		
Simple Profit & Loss Account		£
Sales (or Work Done)		
Less **Expenses**		
Materials Purchased	–	
Premises	1250	
Motor	–	
Office or Administration	–	
Advertising	–	
Accountancy	–	
Profit/Loss on Disposal	–	1250
Profit		-1250

The correct rent to be included in our year is £1,250 (6/12 x £2,500). *NB: With no sales, this gives a loss.*

The Balance Sheet will show a Prepayment of £1,250. This is because although the business paid rent of £2,500, half of which has been included in these accounts, the other half belongs in the following year's accounts. The prepayment effectively puts half of the rent to one side for the following year:

Balance Sheet		
<u>Assets</u>		£
Prepayments		1250
Total Assets	A	**1250**
<u>Liabilities</u>		
Overdraft		2500
Total Liabilities	B	**2500**
Net Assets	A – B	-1250
Capital Account BF		
Plus Profit		-1250
Less Drawings		–
Capital Account CF		-1250

There is an overdraft of £2,500 because the business paid £2,500.

Fiddly bits in a nutshell...

- Accruals are unbilled expenses

- Provisions are possible expenses

- Prepayments are expenses paid in advance

- Accruals and Prepayments appear in the P & L **and** the BS

- A prepayment is deducted from expenses and included in BS as a Debtor

- An accrual is added to expenses and included in the BS as a Creditor

Balance Sheet Example

We have now looked at the P & L and BS in detail and can pull everything together.

In the following example you will find Fixed Tangible Assets (there are no Intangible Assets in our example), Current Assets, and Current Liabilities and Long term Liabilities, and a Capital Account, as well as Accruals and Prepayments, in both BS and P & L. There are also some additional Creditors – PAYE owed to HM Revenue & Customs:

BALANCE SHEET			£
	Assets (What the business owns)		
(Fixed Assets)	Equipment & Furniture	4000	
	less Depreciation (allowance for wearing out)	1000	3000
(Current Assets)	Stock & Work in Progress		3000
(Current Assets)	Debtors (What the business is owed by its customers)		4650
(Current Assets)	Prepayments (Rent)		1250
(Current Assets)	Money in Cash & at the Bank		6400
Total Fixed & Current Assets			**18300**
	Liabilities (What the business owes)		
(Current Liabilities)	Creditors (To its Suppliers and others)		2000
(Current Liabilities)	Accruals (Electricity & Accountancy)		1000
(Current Liabilities)	Provisions		800
(Current Liabilities)	To HM Revenue & Customs for VAT & PAYE		500
(Long Term Liabilities)	Loans		1000
Total Current and Long Term Liabilities			**5300**
(Net Assets)	Net Assets (Value of business) (Total Assets £18300 less total Liabilities £5300)		13000
(Capital Account)	This has come from undrawn business profits -		
	Capital Account BF (Profits of previous years not taken by business owner)		-
	Plus Profit of this year		31000
	Less Drawings (money taken by owner this year)		18000
	Capital Account CF (Value of business remaining)		13000

Notes:

Fixed Assets – Assets that it might take a little while to sell and convert into cash.

Current Assets – Assets that either are actual money or (in theory) could be turned into cash e.g. by selling stock or asking customers to pay their debts.

Current Liabilities – Debts that need to be paid pretty quickly.

Long term Liabilities – Money that the business is paying over a period of time, usually longer than 1 year.

Net Assets have been created by the business trading and making profits (although the net assets may also have been acquired through loans from the owner).

The Capital Account equals the Net Assets and it consists of net profit plus loans/capital introduced less any drawings by the owner.

...cont'd

This is how the P&L looks now after all the new things have been looked at:

Profit and Loss Account	£	£	
Sales		64000	[1]
Opening Stock	Nil		
Plus Purchases	16000		
Total	**16000**		
less Closing Stock	1000	15000	
Gross Profit		49000	GPR 76.5%
Less Overheads			
Wages	7500		[2]
Premises	1650		[3]
Repairs & Maintenance	900		[4]
Motor	2000		
Office or Administration	1500		
Advertising	2000		[5]
Accountancy	1100		
Bad Debt	350		
Depreciation	1000	18000	
Profit		**31000**	

Notes:
1. Sales £60,000 from before plus £4,000 insurance recovery
2. Wages £7,000 plus £500 owed to HMRC for PAYE
3. Premises £1,250 and £400 electricity accrual
4. Repairs £500 less insurance recovery £400 plus provision £800
5. Accountancy £500 paid plus accrual £600

With the BS on p110 and the P & L above, we have a complete set of simple accounts. Normally, accounts will show the previous year's figures alongside the current year's figures so that everyone can compare the two years easily. These previous year figures are often referred to as "Comparatives". As it is the first year of the business, there will not be any comparatives! When we look at Double Entry and the second year of the business, we will see a BS with comparatives.

Cashflow Statement

As well as the Balance Sheet showing you the state of the business at any one time, it is also useful for working out where the cash has been spent i.e. preparing a Cashflow Statement.

From the Balance Sheet it is possible to work out where the money came from and where it went in the year.

Bear in mind that the Balance Sheet has been compiled on the basis of all the paperwork, i.e.:

- Invoices

- Bills

- Receipts

whether or not they have been paid and including expenses that have been incurred but not yet billed.

...cont'd

What actual money was received and how was it spent?

Money in Cash and at the Bank   £

At the beginning of the year	NIL
At the end of the year	6400
Increase (+) or Decrease (–) in Cash at the Bank and In Hand	6400

Where did money come from?

Money from Trading

Profit		31000
Money from other sources		
Loan		1000
Total		**32000**
Less Money not actually received in the year		
Value of WIP included in sales but not actually received in the year	2000	
Money owed to the business (debtors)	4650	6650
Remaining		**25350**
Plus money not actually paid in the year		
Money owed to suppliers & HMRC	2500	
Expenses Accruals (see note 1)	1000	
Repairs Provision	800	
Depreciation	1000	5300
Less Money paid out but not included in Profit		
Rent Prepayment paid but not in Expenses (see note 2)	1250	
Money spent on purchases (see note 3)	1000	2250
Actual Money available		**28400**
How the business has spent this money		
Purchase of assets		4000
Money taken by owner		18000
Remaining (i.e. actual money)		6400

Notes:

1. Expenses Accruals	Electricity	400
	Accountancy	600
	Total	1000

2. Rent Prepayments	Rent paid	2500
	Included in accounts	1250
Prepayment to be included in the following years accounts		1250

3. Cost of Goods Sold (COGS) included in Profit	15000
Plus Closing Stock	1000
Actual Purchases	16000
Included in P & L - COGS	15000
Additional money spent	1000

So closing stock has to be added to arrive at the money spent.

The remaining amount agrees the increase/decrease in Cash at the Bank and In Hand.

By doing this exercise, you have converted the accounts from an accruals basis into cash transactions i.e. real money.

...cont'd

So by taking the accounts and adjusting them for:

- Money not actually received in the year
  (e.g. debtors, WIP)

- Money not actually paid in the year
  (e.g. Creditors, Accruals, Provisions and Depreciation)

- Money paid in the year but not included in the accounts
  (e.g. Prepayments, Closing Stock)

You can arrive at the hard cash the business brought in and see where it went.

Bank Balance Mismatch

Why the bank balance in the Balance Sheet can be different from the Bank Balance on the Bank Statements

The bank balance on the Balance Sheet is not simply the money in the bank at the Balance Sheet date.

It is the money in the bank taking into account all transactions made before the year end **even when they do not appear on the bank statement until later**, e.g. cheques that are written before the year end but do not clear the bank account until after the year end.

Example

Your accounts are for 12 months to 31st March and you write a cheque on 30th March and give it or send it to the person you have written it to; the money for the cheque does not come out of your bank account until 2nd April, two days after your year end.

The bank balance **on the Balance Sheet** is the figure on the bank statement at the year end less the cheque. In other words for accounts purposes, the cheque is considered to be paid out as soon as it has been written **not** when it appears on the bank statement.

The logic of this is that the cheque belongs in the accounts for the year in which it is written not when it eventually appears on the bank statement, which could be up to 6 months after you wrote it if the person you gave it to does not bank it within a reasonable time.

The cheque plays no part in the transactions of the following year and is excluded from the following year's transactions for accounts purposes by accountants.

Accountants like their clients to keep a note of cheques written in the year they are dealing with but have not yet cleared the bank at the year end.

Hot tip

If the business has more than one bank account, e.g. a current account and a savings account, they will sometimes be shown separately on the balance sheet but sometimes be combined, so you may have to add the balances together to see where the bank balance on the balance sheet comes from.

Hot tip

If you cannot find the bank statement figure at the year end in Assets on the Balance Sheet, check that the bank balance is not overdrawn i.e. a negative figure. If it is, you need to look in Liabilities.

...cont'd

A perfect calculation to hand to an accountant would be:

		£
31.3.13	Bank balance per bank statement	6500
30.3.13	Less Chq No 0021	100
31.3.13	**Actual bank balance (for Balance Sheet)**	6400

The same applies if you have **deposited** a cheque and it has not cleared the bank at the year end.

Example
A cheque received and banked on 30th March for £1,000 does not appear on the bank statement until say 3rd April. The bank balance **on the balance sheet** will be £1,000 higher than the bank balance per your bank statement.

As people pay more and more by bank card or internet banking when the transaction often shows on their bank statement on the same day and the use of cheques fades out, the bank balance on the balance sheet will more often be the same as the bank balance on the bank statement.

Control Accounts

There is one other thing you need to be aware of and might be the reason that the accounts include figures that you do not recognise.

Sometimes where businesses do not keep sufficiently detailed records, accountants will check figures they have been given, or at least ensure any discrepancies are correctly dealt with and included in the accounts. They may do this using Control Accounts.

For example, let us take Sales. The figures that affect Sales are:

- Debtors at the start of the year (opening debtors - money still owed by customers from last year)

- Sales invoiced

- Payments made by customers (sales received)

- Debtors at the year end (closing debtors)

The records and accounts should give all these figures and it should be possible to check the closing balances of sales and debtors (closing debtors) at the year end.

The figure for payments made by customers should be reliable if they were all paid into the bank. The bank is the one source of information that accountants almost always check and reconcile.

If we wanted for example to check debtors at the year end we could use the following calculation:

- Start with opening debtors*

- Add sales **recorded** for the year we are dealing with

- Deduct money received from customers in the year

(* we would expect them to be paid in the current year)

We are left then with the money that is still owed by customers at the end of the year i.e. the closing debtors, or just debtors.

If this figure agrees the closing debtors total the business has provided, all is well.

...cont'd

Debtors	£
Opening debtors	NIL
Plus sales invoiced	62000
Total	**62000**
Less payments made by customers and insurance collected in the year (£53000 + £4000)	57000
TOTAL	**5000**
less Bad Debt	350
Balance - Closing Debtors should be	4650

This could equally be presented as:

Debtors	+	–
	£	£
Opening debtors	NIL	
Sales Invoiced	62000	
Money received from customers		57000
Bad Debt		350
Balance (closing debtors)		4650
Total	**62000**	**62000**

Now, if you have totalled up closing debtors and come to a figure of say £5,650 which you have given your accountant, then something is wrong because using the calculation above, closing debtors should be £4,650. Obviously the accountant should investigate this with you.

However, if the amount is not large what he might do is this:

Debtors		
	+	–
	£	£
Opening debtors	NIL	
Sales Invoiced	62000	
Money received from customers		57000
Bad Debt		350
Closing Debtors per business		5650
Balance treated as sales	1000	
Total	**63000**	**63000**

In other words, he works on the basis that if closing debtors are £1,000 higher and the opening debtors are right, and the money received is right then sales must be wrong.

So in the example above sales would be included in the accounts at £63,000 (sales £62,000 + treated as sales £1,000).

This change would be reflected in 2 places in the accounts – debtors are £1,000 higher than the accountant expected and as a result sales are £1,000 higher.

Danger Signs in Accounts

Clearly a **loss** rather than a profit is the obvious danger sign!

In simple terms the business has spent more than it has sold and something is propping up the business e.g.:

1. The owner may have introduced money (capital introduced), or

2. The business may have increased its overdraft or taken out a business loan, or

3. The business may have made its creditors wait longer to be paid

A reduced bank balance or worse, an **overdraft** for the first time, is obviously bad news.

Drawings exceeding profit for the year is another bad sign as it shows the owner is taking out more from the business than it is making. The owner can only do this normally if he has undrawn profits from the past i.e. a Capital Account brought forward figure.

A drop in Gross Profit Ratio/Percentage is another cause for concern.

Any **substantial** increases in any of the expenses should be investigated.

You should also find out what has happened to any expenses that you would expect to be in the accounts but appear not to be.

Any big changes in **any** of the figures should be looked at.

You should ask about any figures that seem just too low or too high.

6 VAT

What is VAT?

VAT has been with us since 1973. It stands for Value Added Tax.

VAT is complicated and makes things difficult for businesses that are registered for VAT.

VAT is a type of "purchase tax". It is added to the cost of goods and services **if** the business supplying the goods and services is VAT registered.

It is administered by HM Revenue & Customs (HMRC).

The current Standard Rate of VAT is 20%. Some goods and services are exempt from tax or "zero rated" which for many purposes is the same thing. There is a special VAT rate for utilities.

If you are **not** VAT registered, VAT forms part of your business costs e.g. goods purchased from a VAT registered business or trader for £100 plus VAT at 20%, total £120, are included in your accounts at £120. It does not matter that some of the £120 is VAT and there is no need to identify it separately:

Bill from ABC Ltd 1.2.11	
	£
Goods	100.00
VAT	20.00
TOTAL	**120.00**

If you are not VAT registered, you can forget that transactions may include VAT and merely include the amount that you pay in your records i.e. £120.00.

If you had sales of £1,000 and the above expenses, your accounts would show a profit of £880:

	£
Sales	1000.00
Expenses	120.00
Paid	**880.00**

If you **are** VAT registered, you **do** need to record VAT separately. You're entitled to claim back VAT that you have paid from HMRC. In the example above you could claim back £20 from

HMRC. As you are claiming back £20 of the £120 you have spent, only £100 is included in the accounts (£120 spent less £20 VAT claimed back).

If you **are** VAT registered, you're required to add VAT to your sales, and must pay this to HMRC. So on a sales invoice of £1,000 if VAT was 20%, you would add VAT of £200 and the total invoice would become £1,200. You have to pay the VAT of £200 to HMRC:

Invoice Date	Supplier	Amount excluding VAT	VAT	Total
		£	£	£
31/12/2012	XYZ Ltd	1000	200	1200

So you can both claim and pay VAT. The VAT you pay is the difference between VAT charged to your customers on your sales invoices and the VAT you have paid on your expenses.

If you had sales of £1,000 plus VAT and purchases of £100 plus VAT, the position would be as follows:

	Invoice Date			Amount excluding VAT	VAT	Total
				£	£	£
	31/12/2012	Customer	XYZ Ltd	1000.00	200.00	1200.00
Less	01/12/2012	Supplier	ABC Ltd	100.00	20.00	120.00
	Total			900.00	180.00	1080.00

You would have to pay VAT of £200 but could claim back VAT of £20. So you would pay £200 less £20 to HMRC, £180.

The accounts would show that you had made a profit of £900:

	£
Sales	1000.00
Purchases	100.00
Profit	900.00

The figures in the accounts are exclusive of VAT.

...cont'd

The VAT you pay of £180 is 20% of the profit (£900 @ 20% = £180). In VAT terms you have bought goods of £100 and "added value" of £900 to them, the VAT on the "added value" is £180 and that is what you pay to HMRC.

The Profit & Loss and Balance Sheet using the figures above would look like this:

Simple Profit & Loss Account	£	£
Sales (or Work Done)		1000
Less Expenses		
Materials Purchased	100	
Premises	–	
Motor	–	
Office or Administration	–	
Advertising	–	
Accountancy	–	
Profit/Loss on Disposal		100
Profit		**900**

The payments on the bank statements will of course include VAT:

Bank Statement	out	in
	£	£
Sales paid		1200
Expenses paid	**120**	
Bank balance at end or closing balance	1080	

Balance Sheet		
Assets		£
Cash at Bank		1080
Total Assets	A	**1080**
Liabilities		
Creditors – VAT owed to HMRC		180
Total Liabilities	B	**180**
Net Assets	A – B	900
Capital Account BF		–
Plus Profit		900
Capital Account CF		**900**

You pay VAT on expenses and declare VAT on sales.

Using HMRC terminology:

- Expenses = Inputs

- Sales = Outputs

In the example above, the £20 VAT on the expenses of £100 is Input Tax. The VAT of £200 on sales is Output Tax.

Hot tip

For future updates see
www.hmrc.gov.uk/vat

Hot tip

Cash Accounting VAT
is more straightforward
and makes record
keeping easier.

When Do You Have to Register for VAT?

You have to register for VAT with HMRC if your turnover (so your total sales) exceeds a certain limit. This changes every year. For 2012/13 (basically April 2012 to April 2013) you will need to register for VAT if your turnover in the previous 12 months exceeds £77,000 at any time in 2012/13.

You have to register in the month after you exceed the registration limit and will be registered for VAT from the beginning of the month after that. E.g. your turnover in the previous 12 months went over the VAT registration in say September. You would have to register with HMRC in October and would be registered for VAT from 1st November.

How to work out VAT - Accruals & Cash Accounting?

A business can choose to account for Input (purchases) and Output (sales) VAT on:

1 Bills issued and received whether or not paid (Accruals), OR

2 Just on bills paid (Cash Accounting)

Paying VAT on Cash Accounting suits a business with slow paying Customers because otherwise the business will pay VAT on sales before it has been paid for them! Paying VAT on Accruals suits a business like a shop which perhaps has no debtors and wants to claim VAT on its bills for expenses before it pays them.

Even if you are a shop and want to be on Accruals VAT to be able to reclaim VAT on bills you have not paid yet, you only get this advantage the first VAT return you do.

The next VAT return you will probably pay the bills that you did not pay for the previous VAT return. You will have already claimed the VAT for these in the previous VAT return. You will claim the VAT on bills unpaid for the second VAT return but the advantage you gained was the first time you did this. Thereafter it is more or less swings and roundabouts.

When Do You Pay VAT?

If you are VAT registered, you have to submit a VAT Return to HM Revenue & Customs at least every three months, so quarterly, and you pay quarterly. You have to do this online.

You don't show every single transaction on the VAT return. The VAT Return is a summary of all the transactions in the quarter.

The VAT Return looks like this:

VAT on Sales and other "outputs" goes in Box 1.

Beware

VAT registered businesses commonly make the mistake of judging how they are doing by how much money they have in the bank and forgetting that some of that money is VAT and belongs to HMRC.

VAT
- At a glance
- Clients
- **Your current client**
  - ▸ **Submit a return**
  - ▸ View submitted returns
  - ▸ Direct Debit
  - ▸ Maintain client
  - ▸ Remove client
- Customer feedback
- FAQs

Submit a return

VAT period

Period:	03 12
Date from:	01 Jan 2012
Date to:	31 Mar 2012
Due date:	07 May 2012

Enter VAT return figures

Enter your figures in the boxes below then click the 'Next' button to continue. For further information on how to complete your return please follow the link Filling in your VAT Return.

Completing your return is different if you use the Flat Rate Scheme. Further information can be found by following the link Flat Rate Scheme for small businesses.

You do not need to enter figures in boxes 3 and 5. These will be automatically calculated and displayed after you click 'Next'.

Please note: The system will time out if you do not use it for 15 minutes. You can save a draft return by clicking the 'Save draft return' button, but please remember to complete and submit the return by the due date.

Please note: Enter values in pounds sterling, including pence, for example 1000.00

* indicates required information

VAT due in this period on **sales** and other outputs (Box 1): *

VAT due in this period on **acquisitions** from other **EC** * **Member States** (Box 2):

Don't forget

VAT on Purchases and other business expenses is called "Input VAT". VAT on Sales is "Output VAT".

VAT reclaimed on purchases and other "inputs" (expenses) goes in Box 4.

The VAT you pay is "Net VAT" in Box 5 above (this is the difference between Box 1 and Box 4).

You have to submit your VAT return online within 30 days of the end of the quarter so if your quarter ends on 31st March, you have to submit and pay the return by 30th April. HMRC like you to pay online too. Most businesses **pay** VAT to HMRC. Some get it back from HMRC.

NOTE
There are other methods of working out VAT e.g. the Flat Rate scheme. These are outside the scope of this book.

Don't forget

VAT belongs to HMRC.

Summary

- Remember if you are VAT registered, accounts are prepared from transactions **excluding** VAT

- If you are not VAT registered, accounts are prepared from transactions **including** VAT

- You have to register for VAT when your turnover in the last 12 months exceeds a certain limit

- If registered, essentially you have to pay HMRC the VAT you have charged on your sales less the VAT that has been charged to you on your purchases and other business expenses

- You can pay VAT on your bills and sales invoices whether or not they have been paid (accruals basis) OR only on the bills and invoices that have been paid (cash accounting)

- VAT returns normally cover three months, a quarter

- You must submit your VAT return online within 30 days of the end of the quarter, and pay them too

7 Companies

A companty protects the business owners from most liabilities that the business may incur – with protection comes responsibiliy

Company Balance Sheets

The Balance Sheet in previous chapters is essentially the same for a Company except:

1 The Capital Account Brought Forward (BF) is referred to as Reserves or Retained Profit

2 The owner or owners also have shares and these appear on the BS. Both are added together and the total is called 'Shareholders Funds'

So in addition to the Reserves/Retained Profits on a Company Balance Sheet, there will also be shareholdings on the Balance Sheet (see below).

Example

John wants to run his business as a Limited Company.

He forms the Company by registering it at Companies House and undertaking to pay £1 for 1 share worth £1, and appoints himself director. If the Balance Sheet was prepared at the end of the first day the Company was formed, it would look like this:

Balance Sheet at Day 1		
Assets		£
Cash or Bank Balance	A	1
Liabilities		
None	B	NIL
Net Assets	A-B	1
Capital Account (Reserves) BF		NIL
Share		1
Shareholders Funds	B	1

Net assets match shareholders funds.

We will use the same P & L for the company as on p112 but the P & L will also show tax and profit after tax. The owners drawings would be accounted for in a special account called the Directors Current or Loan Account which appears on the Balance Sheet.

The director/shareholder could decide to pay out the £18,000 drawings as salary and this would be treated the same as the salaries of other employees i.e. as an expense of the business.

Alternatively the director/shareholder could decide to pay out the £18,000 as dividends.

A dividend is a distribution of profit to the shareholders paid according to their shareholdings. So if there were two shareholders each with one share and the directors decided to make one payment of £18,000 as a dividend, each shareholder would get £9,000. Directors would have to hold an official meeting to declare the dividend and keep Minutes of the meeting. The Minutes would say that the Company had made a profit and had voted a dividend of £9,000 per share. So shareholders would get £9,000 for each share they had.

Our company only has 1 share, so if £18,000 is paid as dividends once in the year, the Minutes would show that the Company had decided to pay a dividend of £18,000 per share.

A Company can pay dividends monthly if it wishes. So it could pay £1,500 every month. In which case each month the Directors would have to hold a meeting and vote a dividend of £1,500 each share. At the end of the year 12 dividends would have been paid of £1,500 per share totalling £18,000.

Dividends are shown in the Company's P & L as a deduction from profit after tax.

So the Profit and Loss for a Company would look like this:

	£
Profit on ordinary activities before taxation:	31000
Less Tax on profit on ordinary activities (say 20%):	6200
Profit for the financial year after tax:	24800
Less Dividend	18000
Retained Profit for the year	6800

As this is a P & L for a company, the tax is shown. Company tax is called Corporation Tax.

Beware

The Company may pay a dividend out of profits and the Company must check it has made a profit before a dividend is paid.

133

...cont'd

After dividends and tax are taken into account, the BS will look like this:

BALANCE SHEET			Year Ended 31st March
			£
	Assets (What the business owns)		
(Fixed Assets)	Equipment & Furniture	4000	–
	less Depreciation	1000	3000
(Current Assets)	Stock & Work in Progress		3000
(Current Assets)	Debtors (customers)		4650
(Current Assets)	Prepayments (Rates)		1250
(Current Assets)	Money in Cash & at the Bank[1]		6401
	Total Fixed & Current Assets		**18301** A
	Liabilities (What the business owes)		
(Current Liabilities)	Creditors (owed to Suppliers and others)		2000
(Current Liabilities)	Accruals (e.g. Electricity)		1000
(Current Liabilities)	Provisions		800
(Current Liabilities)	To HMRC for VAT, PAYE & Corporation Tax[2]		6700
(Long Term Liabilities)	Loans		1000
	Total Current and Long Term Liabilities		**11500** B
	Net Assets (Value of business)		**6801** A-B
	Capital & Reserves (Undrawn profits and share capital)		
	Reserves BF (Profits of previous years retained by Company)		–
	Plus Profit of this year		6800
	Plus Share Capital		1
	Shareholders Funds		**6801**

1. *This includes £1 paid for 1 share*

2. *The amount owed to HMRC is £500 for PAYE and £6200 for Corporation Tax (see p87)*

Directors' Responsibilities

The directors are appointed to act on behalf of the shareholders to run the day-to-day affairs of the business and are directly accountable to the shareholders. In small companies, the directors are often also the shareholders. The directors are often referred to as the Board (of directors). Directors will meet and make decisions or resolutions by voting.

Summary of company directors' responsibilities

Company directors have a general responsibility to act in a way they consider, in good faith, would be most likely to promote the success of the company for the benefit of its shareholders as a whole (S172 Companies Act 2006).

They are responsible for:

- Ensuring Companies House have accurate and up-to-date information about the company and its officers

- Complying with the law e.g. concerning health and safety

- The actions of employees of the company

Directors must deliver the following, on behalf of the company, to Companies House:

- The annual return

- The annual accounts

- Notification of any change in the company's officers or in their personal details

- Notification of a change to the company's registered office

Company officers are its directors and company secretary, if it has one (it is no longer a requirement for a company to have a company secretary).

The annual return confirms the company's shares, officers, registered address, etc.

If there is a company secretary he/she will often file everything necessary with Company House. However ultimate responsibility remains with the company's directors.

Legal Requirements for Company Accounts

Who should prepare a Company's accounts?
The directors are responsible for ensuring accounts are prepared for each financial year.

Does a Company have to use an accountant?
There is no requirement for companies to use an accountant to prepare their accounts. However, directors almost always get professional accountants to prepare them.

What period must they cover?
A company's first accounts start on the date of incorporation, not the first day of trading, and must normally cover at least 12 months to the end of the month so a Company incorporated on 15th May 2012 must prepare accounts for the period 15.5.12 – 31.5.13.

Subsequent accounts run from the day after the previous accounts ended and normally finish 12 months later so for the example above, 1.6.13 to 31.5.14.

What should company accounts consist of?
Generally, accounts must include:

1. A profit and loss account (or income and expenditure account if the company is not trading for profit)

2. A balance sheet signed by a director showing the printed name of the director who is signing the balance sheet on behalf of the company

3. Notes to the accounts

4. A directors' report that shows the printed name of the approving director

What notes to the accounts might be needed?
Directors' salaries and pension contributions

If the director(s) receive a salary (remuneration), the total remuneration should be included in a note to the accounts. Any pension contributions made for the directors are shown separately:

CY = Current Year   PY = Previous Year

	CY	PY
	£	£
Directors' remuneration:	18000	18000
Value of directors' pension contributions:	-	-
Total:	**18000**	**18000**
The number of Directors accruing pension benefits was:	1	1

Directors' Loans

If the directors have had loans from the company, details should be included in a note to the accounts.

For each director and for each loan, the note should show:

- The amount of the loan
- The interest being charged if any
- The main conditions of the loan e.g. when it is to be repaid
- Any repayments made in the year
- The opening and closing balances of loans (the amount of the loans at the beginning of the year and at the end)
- The maximum amount owed by each director in the year

(S413 Companies Act 2006)

What should be in the directors' report?

The directors' report should include a description of the company's principal activities, a review of the business and an indication of future developments.

Do company accounts have to be audited?

Only large companies with turnover or assets of several million pounds have to have their accounts audited.

The accounts of companies that are exempt from audit must carry the following statement:

Audit Exemption Statement

For the year ending ....(dd/mm/yyyy) the company was entitled to exemption from audit under section 477 of the Companies Act 2006 relating to small companies.

Directors' responsibilities:

- the members have not required the company to obtain an audit of its accounts for the year in question in accordance with section 476

- the directors acknowledge their responsibilities for complying with the requirements of the Act with respect to accounting records and the preparation of accounts

- these accounts have been prepared in accordance with the provisions applicable to companies subject to the small companies' regime

The information above applies to "small" companies. "Very large" companies are subject to more regulation.

Who can sign the accounts?

The company's board of directors must approve the accounts before they send them to the shareholders (also known as members):

1 A director must sign the **balance sheet** on behalf of the board, their name should be printed amd any exemptions statements should appear above the director's signature

2 A director or the company secretary must sign **the directors' report** on behalf of the board and their name should be printed. Any statement about acounts being prepared under the small companies regime must appear above the signature, and

3 If the company has to attach an auditor's report to the accounts, the report must include the auditor's signature and their name must be printed

Does the Company have to hold a meeting of its shareholders to approve the accounts (an annual general meeting)?

There is no longer a statutory requirement for private companies to lay their accounts before members at a general meeting but some company's Articles may specify that the company must still do so. The shareholders may pass a special resolution to remove that provision if they wish.

Who must receive a copy of the Companies accounts?

Every company must send a copy of its annual accounts for each financial year to every shareholder. A copy may be provided electronically but shareholders have a right to a paper copy.

Do a full set of the accounts need to be sent to Companies House?

You can simply file a copy of the full accounts that you have already prepared for the members/shareholders at Companies House. However, small and medium-sized companies may file an abbreviated version of those accounts which is essentially just the balance sheet.

...cont'd

140

What names and signatures should be given on the accounts for filing with Companies House?

Copies of accounts sent to Companies House must meet the following requirements:

1 The copy of the Balance Sheet must show the printed name of the director who signed it on behalf of the board and be signed by that director

2 If a copy of the directors' report is included, it must show the printed name of the director or company secretary who signed the report although it does not need to be signed

3 If the company chooses not to include a copy of the directors' report and/or a copy of the company's profit and losses, the balance sheet must also contain the following statement: 'The accounts have been delivered in accordance with the provisions applicable to companies subject to the small companies' regime.'

Sample Company Accounts

A full set of Company Accounts might look like this:

(We will call the company Luxury Windows Limited)

Cover page

<u>**Luxury Windows Limited**</u>

Company Registration Number: 03456789 (England and Wales)

Report of the Directors and Unaudited Financial Statements

Period of accounts

Start date: 1st April 2013

End date: 31st Mar 2014

1

Contents

<u>**Luxury Windows Limited**</u>

Contents of the Financial Statements for the
Period Ended 31st Mar 2014

Company Information

Report of the Directors

Profit and Loss Account

Balance Sheet

Notes to the Financial Statements

2

Company Information

<u>**Luxury Windows Limited**</u>

Company Information for the Period Ended 31st Mar 2014

Director: J Black

Company secretary: D Smith

Registered office: Street, Town, County Post Code

Company Registration Number: 03456789 (England and Wales)

3

Directors Report

Luxury Windows Limited

Directors' Report for the Period Ended 31st Mar 2014

The directors present their report with the financial statements of the company for the period ended 31st Mar 2014

Principal activities

The principal activity of the company in the period under review was: window sales and installation

Directors

The directors shown below have held office during the whole of the period from 1st April 2013 to 31st Mar 2014

J Black

Political and charitable donations, for the period under review and previous period

There were no charitable donations during the year (2013: Nil). No contributions to political organisations were made during the year.

The above report has been prepared in accordance with the special provisions in part 15 of the Companies Act 2006.

This report was approved by the board of directors on (date)

And Signed On Behalf Of The Board By:

Name: J Black

Status: Director

4

Profit & Loss

Luxury Windows Limited

Profit and Loss Account for the Period Ended 31st Mar 2014

	Notes	2014 £	2013 £
Turnover:	1	63,350	64,000
Cost of sales:		15,000	15,000
Gross Profit/(Loss):		48,350	49,000
Distribution costs:		-	-
Administrative expenses:		18,860	18,000
Other operating income:		-	-
Profit/(Loss) on disposal of fixed assets:		-	-
Operating Profit/(Loss):		29,490	31,000
Interest receivable and similar:		-	-
Interest payable and similar:		100	-
Profit/(Loss) on ordinary activities before taxation:		29,390	31,000
Tax on profit on ordinary activities:		5,878	6,200
Profit/(Loss) for the financial year after taxation:		23,512	24,800

The notes form part of these financial statements

Luxury Windows Limited
Statement of total recognised gains and losses for the period ended 31 Mar 2014

The company does not have any gains and losses other than Profit and Loss for the period to report.

5

...cont'd

Balance Sheet

Luxury Windows Limited

Balance sheet for the Period Ended 31st Mar 2014

	Notes	2014 £	2013 £
Fixed assets			
Intangible fixed assets:		Nil	Nil
Tangible fixed assets:	5	2,250	3,000
Investments:		Nil	Nil
Total fixed assets:		2,250	3,000
Current assets			
Stocks & WIP:		3,000	3,000
Debtors:	6	7,350	5,900
Cash at bank and in hand:		11,851	6,401
Total current assets:		22,201	15,301
Creditors			
Creditors - amounts falling due within one year:	7	11,538	9,700
Net current assets:		10,663	5,601
Total assets less current liabilities:		12,913	8,601
Creditors - amounts falling due after more than one year:		600	1,000
Provision for liabilities:	9	Nil	800
Net assets:		12,313	6,801
Capital and reserves			
Called up share capital:	10	1	1
Profit and loss account:	11	12,312	6,800
Total shareholders funds:		12,313	6,801

These accounts have been prepared in accordance with the special provisions in part 15 of Companies Act 2006 relating to small companies and in accordance with the Financial Reporting Standard for Smaller Entities (effective April 2008).

For the year ending 31st May 2014 the company was entitled to exemption from audit, in accordance with sections 475 and 477 of the Companies Act 2006 relating to small companies and no notice has been deposited under Section 476 of the Act.

The directors acknowledge their responsibilities for complying with the requirements of the Companies Act 2006 with respect to accounting records and the preparation of accounts.

The financial statements were approved by the Board of Directors on (date).

SIGNED ON BEHALF OF THE BOARD BY:

Name: J Black

Status: Director

The notes form part of these financial statements

6

Notes to the Financial Statements

<u>Luxury Windows Limited</u>

Notes to the Financial Statements
for the Period Ended 31st Mar 2014

1. Accounting policies

Basis of preparation
The financial statements have been prepared under the historical cost convention and in accordance with the Financial Reporting Standard for Smaller Entities (Effective April 2008)

Turnover
The turnover shown in the profit and loss account represents revenue earned during the period, exclusive of VAT

7 cont...

Tangible fixed assets – Depreciation
Depreciation is provided, after taking account of any grants receivable, at the following annual rates in order to write off each asset over its estimated useful life.
Freehold buildings – 2% on cost or revalued amounts
Plant and machinery – 15% on cost
Fixtures and fittings – 10% on cost
Motor vehicles – 25% on cost
No depreciation is provided on freehold land

Intangible fixed assets
Intangible fixed assets (including purchased goodwill and patents) are amortised at rates calculated to write off the assets on a straight basis over their estimated useful economic lives, not to exceed twenty years.

Stocks
Stocks and work-in-progress are valued at the lower of cost and net realisable value, after making due allowance for obsolete and slow moving items.

Deferred taxation
Deferred tax is recognised in respect of all timing differences that have originated but not reversed at the balance sheet date.

Hire purchase and leasing commitments
Assets obtained under hire purchase contracts or finance leases are capitalised in the balance sheet.
Those held under hire purchase contracts are depreciated over their estimated useful lives. Those held under finance leases are depreciated over their estimated useful lives or the lease term, whichever is the shorter.
The interest element of these obligations is charged to the profit and loss account over the relevant period.
The capital element of the future payments is treated as a liability.
Rentals paid under operating leases are charged to the profit and loss account on a straight line basis over the period of the lease.

Research and Development
Expenditure on research and development is written off in the year in which it is incurred.

7

2. Directors' remuneration

	2014	2013
	£	£
Directors' remuneration:	Nil	Nil
Value of directors' pension contributions:	Nil	Nil
Total:	Nil	Nil

3. Employees

	2014	2013
	£	£
Wages and salaries:	7,000	7,000
Social security costs:	1,600	1,500
Pension costs:	Nil	Nil
Total staff costs:	8,600	8,500

4. Dividends

Dividend on ordinary shares of £18000 paid in period ended 31st Mar 2014

5. Tangible fixed assets

	Land and Buildings £	Plant and machinery £	Fixtures and fittings £	Office equipment £	Motor vehicles £	Total £
Cost						
At 1 April 2013:	-	-	-	-	4,000	4,000
Additions:	-	-	-	-	-	-
Disposals:	-	-	-	-	-	-
At 31st Mar 2014:	-	-	-	-	4,000	4,000
Depreciation						
At 1 April 2013:	-	-	-	-	1,000	1,000
Charge for year:	-	-	-	-	750	750
On disposals:	-	-	-	-	-	-
At 31st Mar 2014:	-	-	-	-	1,750	1,750
Net book value						
At 31st Mar 2014:	-	-	-	-	2,250	2,250
At 31st Mar 2013	-	-	-	-	3,000	3,000

8 cont...

Note: the Net Book Value (NBV) at 31st March 2014 is shown before the NBV at 31st March 2013.

Included in plant and machinery are only assets held under hire purchase contracts.

The net book value of these assets amounted to £Nil (2013: £Nil)

6. Debtors

	2014 £	2013 £
Trade debtors:	6,000	4,650
Other debtors:	Nil	Nil
Prepayments and accrued income:	1,350	1,25
Total:	7,350	5,900

7. Creditors: amounts falling due within one year

	2014 £	2013 £
Bank loans and overdrafts:	Nil	Nil
Amounts due under finance leases and hire purchase contracts:	Nil	Nil
Trade creditors:	4,000	2,000
Taxation and social security:	600	500
Accruals and deferred income:	1,060	1,800
Other creditors:	Nil	Nil
Total:	5,660	4,300

8. Borrowings

The following loans are included within creditors:

Repayable	2014 £	2013 £
Within one year:	Nil	Nil
Between one and five years:	600	1,000
Over five years:	Nil	Nil
Total:	600	1,000

8 cont...

9. Provisions for liabilities

Provisions	2014 £	2013 £
At 1st April :	800	Nil
Movements to:	Nil	800
Movements from:	800	Nil
At 31st Mar :	Nil	800

Movements to: are transfers from the profit and loss account.

Movements from: are utilisations of the provision

10. Share capital

Allotted, called up and paid	2014	2013
Ordinary shares of £1 each	1	1

11. Reserves/Retained profit

Retained profit reconciliation	£	£
Reserves at 1st April :	6,800	Nil
Profit for year:	23,512	24,800
Equity dividends paid:	18,000	18,000
Retained profit at 31st Mar	12,312	6,800

12. Related party transactions

The ultimate controlling party during the period:

J Black holds 100% of the issued share capital and is deemed the ultimate controlling party.

13. Contingent liabilities

In the previous year the company received a £800 claim for damages to adjoining premises.

The Company believed there was some doubt about its liability but to save the costs of litigation has paid for the repairs.

14. Post balance sheet events

There were no post balance sheet events

8

...cont'd

	2014			2013
	£	£	£	£
Sales		63350		64000
Opening Stock	1000		Nil	
Plus Purchases	16000		16000	
Total	17000		16000	
less Closing Stock	2000	15000	1000	15000
Gross Profit		48350		49000
GPR	(76.3%)		(76.3%)	
Less Overheads				
Wages	8600		7500	
Premises	3040		1650	
Repairs & Maintenance	100		900	
Motor	2000		2000	
Office or Administration	1750		1500	
Advertising	2000		2000	
Accountancy	620		1100	
Bad Debts	0		350	
Finance Charges	100		0	
Depreciation	750	18960	1000	18000
Profit		29390		31000

Notes:

1. The figures for the second year, 2014, include payment of the tax due for 2013 so the creditor for corporation tax for 2013 of £6,200 at the end of 2013 is paid and the bank balance at the end of 2014 is £6,200 less as a result.

2. The figures for 2014 include the creditor for corporation tax for 2014 of £5,878 so creditors are £11,538 (trade creditors £4000 + accruals £1,060 + PAYE £600 + corporation tax creditor £5,878).

Anyone can obtain a copy of the accounts filed with Companies House by paying a small fee to Companies House.

Limited Liability Partnerships are similar to companies in that they have to file accounts with Companies House. They are not commonly used by ordinary businesses. A limited company is more commonly known to be limited in liability and more easily understood. Limited Liability Partnerships (LLP) tend to be used by professionals like solicitors and accountants. Accountancy fees for LLPs are higher. Businesses should take professional advice on whether or not they trade as an LLP.

Companies House Deadlines

Deadlines and fines

Accounts

Accounts have to be filed with Companies House within nine months after the company's financial year ends although it can be slightly earlier for the first Company accounts.

Anyone can look up a company on the Companies House website and see the deadline for filing accounts.

If accounts are late, fines currently range from £150 to £1,500 and double if accounts are late two years running. These fines are criminal and we have known of cases where company directors have been threatened with arrest for non payment.

Companies House are bringing in more than £50m per year from these penalties and they do not accept excuses for accounts being late. They take the line that if something like bad weather or sudden sickness prevented accounts being filed on time, the company should not have left it till the last minute.

Returns

Companies also have to file a return every year. Again anyone can check the Companies House website for when this needs to be done although Companies House say that they send out reminders in good time. Our experience is that these do not always arrive.

If a return is not submitted in time, Companies House write to the Directors warning that failure to submit the return will result in the company being struck off the company register i.e. the company will cease to exist. If this happens all company bank accounts are frozen and if the company is not restored to the register (a costly procedure), the money in the bank accounts eventually passes to the Crown. Indeed all the company assets are effectively frozen and it is a criminal offence should the director dispose of them.

Summary

- The duties of a director of a limited company are laid down by law

- Directors must run the company for the benefit of all its shareholders

- The directors of a company are responsible for complying with company law even if they delegate to someone else, e.g. company secretary or an accountant

- Directors must submit annual returns and accounts to Companies House, and notify Companies House of any changes in the company's officers (or their details), and the company's registered office

- A company's accounts must be in a particular format and contain notes about directors' salaries and loans

- If the accounts are in the wrong format, they will be rejected by Companies House

- Accounts and returns need to be submitted to Companies House by specific deadlines or the directors will be fined and may lose the company and its assets

- Business profits for tax may be different to the profits in the accounts

- A company Balance Sheet is different to the BS for a sole trader or partnership. It shows shareholdings

- The Capital Account BF is called Reserves or Retained Profits and together with the company's shareholdings is referred to as Shareholder Funds

- Shareholder funds equal the company's net assets

...cont'd

- The Reserves or Retained Profits at year-end are:

  – Reserves or Retained Profits BF

  – Plus Profit of the year (after any dividends and tax paid)

- Tax and dividends will be shown in the company P & L

- Directors/shareholders can take their drawings as a loan, as a salary or as a dividend(s)

- Before paying a dividend the directors must check the company is profitable

8 Double Entry

Double Entry is as much about symmetry as it is about figures

What is Double Entry?

Can one talk about accounts without mentioning double entry?

Double entry bookkeeping is a method of keeping books and records and preparing accounts that ensures nothing is missed. The accounts are self checking because they are self balancing.

Double entry system is at least 600 years old and may be considerably older.

Why do you need to know about double entry bookkeeping?

All accounts are based on double entry. You have had a flavour of that when we changed the early balance sheets. Everything resulted in two changes.

Having a general understanding of double entry will help you with discussions with your bookkeeper or accountant. It will stop you feeling that they are talking a different language.

Although double entry is built into software packages and done for you, if printouts are laid out in "debits" and "credits", you will obviously need to know the basics of double entry to have any chance of understanding them.

If you can summarise the double entry (and complete a "Trial Balance"), you could prepare your own accounts or at least a first draft of your accounts for your accountant. Even if you just gave your accountant a summary or a Trial Balance it should help keep your accountancy costs down.

If you can prepare a Trial Balance, you will have a much greater understanding of what is in your accounts.

If you do not mind not understanding Double Entry and having no idea what a trial balance is or a debit or credit, and want to leave it completely to your accountant then you could skip the section on Double Entry. WE DO NOT ADVISE THAT.

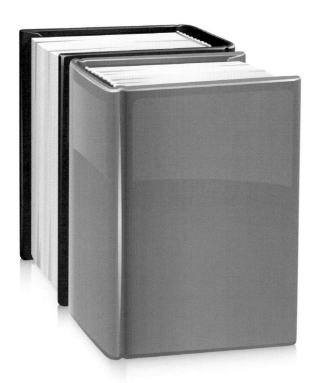

The sections in this book on Double Entry are straightforward and have simple examples. The same figures are used again and again wherever possible and they build up to produce the accounts that you have already seen. There is also a set of accounts for the following year so you can see accounts with comparatives and understand how items affect both years.

Starting Double Entry

Debits and credits

In Double Entry bookkeeping, for every transaction there are two entries: a Debit **and** a Credit.

This is the key to double entry. **Every** transaction involves **two** entries in the accounts.

Each transaction is entered in its own category or account ("nominal" in accountancy language). Each account is commonly shown like this.

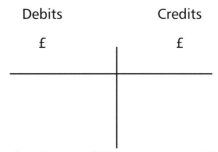

This is often referred to as a "T" account with a Debit side and a Credit side.

So receiving £10 in cash for goods sold would come under the category of **Sales** and the other category involved i.e. **Cash**. So two entries are involved (double entry) and in one category the transaction will be a Debit and in the other category it will be a Credit.

In fact the transaction under **Sales** will be a Credit.

Sales		
	Debit	**Credit**
Description	£	£
Cash		10

And the transaction in **Cash** will be a Debit:

Cash		Debit	Credit
		Debit	Credit
Description		£	£
Sales		10	

Here we specified which was a Debit and which a Credit.

How do you determine whether a transaction is a Debit or Credit?

How can you check that you have them right i.e. you haven't called a Debit a Credit by mistake?

This question is the essence of double entry bookkeeping.

We recommend using a simple debit or credit grid.

Debit or Credit Grid (Dr/Cr Grid)

Debits	Credits
Expenses	Sales
Assets	Liabilities

So in our example, Sales are a Credit. Cash is an Asset and a Debit.

Also, if you can be sure that one of the two transactions is a Debit or Credit, the other transaction (i.e. the other double entry) must be the opposite. Therefore if you remember that Sales are a Credit, the entry in the Cash category must be a Debit.

It is a similar position if the Sales had been a bank transfer.

The only difference would be that instead of the other category being Cash, it would be Bank:

Sales		
	Debit	**Credit**
Description	£	£
Bank		10

Bank		
	Debit	**Credit**
Description	£	£
Sales	10	

£10 has been paid into the bank. The money in the bank has gone up by £10. But it is a Debit?

It will be illogical to many people that money going into the bank is a Debit because when we talk about our bank account we think of money going in as being "credited".

This is because people do not realise that they are using bank terminology i.e. they are looking at double entry as though they were the bank.

From the bank's point of view, the money paid into a bank account is a liability. The bank owes the customer this money. Therefore, it is a **credit** to the bank.

BUT the business is not the bank and for the business the position is reversed. Money going into the bank for the business is an Asset and a Debit (see Dr/Cr Grid above for the business).

If you remember this, it will help you work out whether any transaction is a Debit or a Credit.

If the business pays for something, for example, with a business cheque or debit card, then money in the bank (an Asset) is reducing and this will be a Credit to the bank account. So having got that right, whatever it paid for, i.e. the other entry (double entry) must be a Debit.

So if the business paid £10 for stationery with a bank card, this would be the position:

Bank		
	Debit	Credit
Description	£	£
Stationery		10

Money in the bank is going down (it is like a Liability in the Dr/Cr Grid). It is a Credit.

Stationery		
	Debit	**Credit**
Description	£	£
Bank	10	

As the double entry for the Bank category above is a Credit and provided you are happy with that, what has been bought, i.e. the Stationery, must be a Debit!

...cont'd

Alternatively, you could have looked at the Dr/Cr Grid and worked out that Stationery is an Expense of the business and so is a Debit. All Expenses are Debits.

Debits	Credits
Expenses	Sales
Assets	Liabilities

There are several ways of working out which transaction is a Debit and which is a Credit and if you find your own, foolproof method then stick with it.

Let us look at some other examples.

Let us say the business buys Stationery costing £100 from Pens International Ltd but it does not have to pay them for 30 days, so it is buying the goods on credit.

Firstly the transaction still involves the purchase of Stationery, so one category will be Stationery. Stationery is an Expense of the business and so using the Dr/Cr Grid, it is a Debit:

Stationery		
	Debit	Credit
Description	£	£
Pens International Ltd	100	

The other category (or account) is Pens International Ltd. The business owes them money so this is a liability of the business.

Using the Dr/Cr Grid above, a Liability is a Credit, so the category for Pens International Ltd will look like this:

Pens International Ltd		
	Debit	Credit
Description	£	£
Stationery		10

So, there are two entries, one in Stationery category (a Debit) and the other in Pens International Limited (a Credit).

Let us look at how the transactions in our accounts above would be treated using double entry.

You can check which entries are Debits and which Credits against the Dr/Cr Grid:

Debits	Credits
Expenses	Sales
Assets	Liabilities

Remember money in the bank account or going into the bank account will be an Asset of the business and therefore a Debit. Money going out of the bank account will be a Liability of the business and therefore a Credit.

...cont'd

For the six transactions below, we have given you the first category of the Double Entry - see if you can work out what the second category is and whether the transactions are Debits or Credits.

Have a go at completing Transaction 1 and check the answer on p169. Then, complete transcations 2-6. Check answers to these on p170-173.

To start you off, in Transaction 1 we have given you the first category and the second category (the other Double Entry). Decide whether £53,000 is a Debit or a Credit in each category.

1 Business Transaction Sales of £53,000 made to Customers paid for by bank transfers
First Category is **Sales**.
Is it a Debit or a Credit? (see Dr/Cr Grid)

Category - Sales		
	Debit	Credit
Description	£	£
Bank		

The Description "Bank" points to the other part of the Double Entry i.e. Bank.

The second category, therefore, is Bank. Is it a Debit or a Credit?

Category - Bank		
	Debit	Credit
Description	£	£
Sales		

Again the Description points you to where the other part of the Double Entry is to be found so the two Categories involved are "Sales" and "Bank".

If you're not sure whether you have got the Debits and Credits right, have a look at p169. Otherwise, carry on and have a go at Transactions 2-6.

We have given you the first category for numbers 2 – 6. The second category will be one of the categories below:

- Bank

- Debtors (various)

- ABC Ltd (creditors)

2   Sales of £5,000 made to various customers on credit
So the customers are Debtors
First category is **Sales**
Is it a Debit or a Credit?

Category - Sales		
	Debit	Credit
Description	£	£
?		

What is the second category (the other part of the Double Entry)? Is it a Debit or a Credit?

Category - ?		
	Debit	Credit
Description	£	£
?		

£2,000 stock (goods for you to sell) bought from a Supplier (ABC Ltd) on credit

First Category is Purchases which are an Expense.

Debit or Credit?

Category - Purchases		
	Debit	Credit
Description	£	£
?		

Second Category?

Debit or Credit?

Category - ?		
	Debit	Credit
Description	£	£
?		

4. Van purchased for £4,000 with a cheque
First Entry is Vehicles
Is it a Debit or a Credit?

Category - Vehicles		
	Debit	**Credit**
Description	£	£
?		

Second Category?

Debit or Credit?

Category - ?		
	Debit	**Credit**
Description	£	£
?		

5. Vehicle expenses totalling £2,000 paid by bank debit card
First Category is Motor
Is it a Debit or a Credit?

Category - Motor		
	Debit	**Credit**
Description	£	£
?		

...cont'd

Second Category?

Debit or Credit?

Category - ?		
	Debit	**Credit**
Description	£	£
?		

6 Bank Loan transfer £1,000 to the main business bank current account.
First Category is Bank Loan.
Is it a Debit or a Credit?

Category - Bank Loan		
	Debit	**Credit**
Description	£	£
?		

Second Category?

Debit or Credit?

Category - ?		
	Debit	**Credit**
Description	£	£
?		

You can now check whether you got these right, especially, whether you had the Debits and Credits the right way round.

The answers are (and for completeness all 1 – 6 are shown):

1 Business Transaction Sales of £53,000 made to Customers paid for by bank transfers
First Category is **Sales**
And is a **Credit**

Category - Sales		
	Debit	Credit
Description	£	£
Bank		53000

The Description tells you where the other part of the Double Entry can be found.

The Second Category (the other part of the Double Entry) is **Bank.**

Money is coming into the bank and so is an Asset and so a **Debit.**

In any case, if the first Category is a Credit, the Double Entry must be a Debit, so:

Category - Bank		
	Debit	Credit
Description	£	£
Sales	53000	

Again the Description tells you where the other part of the Double Entry is to be found so the two Categories involved are **"Sales"** and **"Bank".**

...cont'd

2   Sales of £5,000 made to various Customers on credit
First Category is **Sales**
And is a **Credit**

Category - Sales		
	Debit	Credit
Description	£	£
Debtors (various)		5000

Second Category (the other part of the Double Entry) is **Debtors.**

The Double Entry must be a **Debit** if you worked out that the first entry is a Credit.

But in any case Debtors are an Asset. Assets are Debits (per the Dr/Cr Grid).

Category - Debtors		
	Debit	Credit
Description	£	£
Sales	5000	

The Description points to the other Double Entry i.e. Sales so the Double Entries are **Sales** and **Debtors.**

3   £2,000 stock (goods for you to sell) bought from a Supplier (ABC Ltd) on credit
First Category is **Purchases**
And is a **Debit** – see the Dr/Cr Grid (Purchases are Expenses of the business)

Category - Purchases		
	Debit	Credit
Description	£	£
ABC Ltd	2000	

Second Category is ABC Ltd or **Creditors**.

Creditors are a Liability and therefore a **Credit.**

Category - ABC Ltd (Creditors)		
	Debit	Credit
Description	£	£
Purchases		2000

The Description points to the other Double Entry i.e. Purchases and so the **two** categories involved in the Double Entry are **Purchases** and **ABC Ltd** (Creditors).

4 Van purchased for £4,000 with a cheque
First Entry is **Vehicles**
And is a **Debit** because Vehicles are an **Asset** – see the Dr/Cr Grid

Category - Vehicles		
	Debit	Credit
Description	£	£
Bank	4000	

Second Entry is **Bank**

The entry is a **Credit** because it is money going out of the Bank (treated as a Liability).

Category - Bank		
	Debit	Credit
Description	£	£
Vehicles		4000

The Double Entries are **Vehicles** and **Bank.**

5 Vehicle expenses totalling £2,000 paid by bank debit card
First Category is **Motor**
And is a Debit because it is an **Expense**

Category - Motor		
	Debit	Credit
Description	£	£
Bank	2000	

Second Category is **Bank.**

The entry is a **Credit** because it is money going out of the Bank (treated as a Liability).

Category - Bank		
	Debit	Credit
Description	£	£
Motor		2000

The Double Entries are **Motor** and **Bank.**

6 Bank Loan transfer £1,000
First Category is **Bank Loan**
And is **Credit** because it is a Liability

Category - Bank Loan		
	Debit	**Credit**
Description	£	£
Bank		1000

Second Category is **Bank**. The money has been paid into the main bank account.

It is a **Debit** as it is money coming into the main bank account and an Asset.

Category - Bank		
	Debit	**Credit**
Description	£	£
Bank Loan	1000	

The Double Entries are **Bank Loan** and **Bank.** You may not have got No 6 right. It depends on whether you realised that the bank loan was a separate category. It has to be. There are **ALWAYS** two categories and entries in Double Entry.

Summary

- In Double Entry, there are **ALWAYS** two transactions, a Debit and a Credit

- Use this Dr/Cr Grid to help you decide which is which

Debits	Credits
Expenses	Sales
Assets	Liabilities

- Money going into the bank is always a Debit, the opposite probably to how you may have thought about it

- Double Entry is about taking **CARE**. If you **ALWAYS** make two entries per transaction, one a Debit and the other a Credit, you will not be looking through the figures later wondering where you went wrong

- Double Entry is as much about symmetry as it is about figures

9 Nominal Accounts

There is no mystery about nominal accounts. They are just a way of keeping things tidy in their own compartments

Overview

In Double Entry bookkeeping, in theory, there are at least three sets of accounting records:

1   Sales ledger for customers' personal accounts (an account for each customer)

2   Purchase ledger for suppliers' personal accounts (an account for each supplier)

3   Nominal ledger for all other accounts - expenses, assets, loans etc

In practice, there is really only one set of accounting records – Nominal Accounts.

The Nominal Accounts are the various Categories making up the accounts. They are a gathering together of all transactions in the same category for the whole year.

All goods sold to different customers are grouped together in the Sales Nominal account.

All goods purchased from different suppliers are grouped together in the Purchases Nominal account.

Other business expenditure, e.g. Stationery & Postage is put together in the Stationery & Postage Nominal account.

The Categories in the examples above are in simple terms, the Nominals.

Categories = Nominals

Trial Balance

The Trial Balance is a summary of all the Nominal Accounts. It is a listing of all the Debit and all the Credit balances on the Nominal Accounts. If you have always made two entries, one a Debit and one a Credit, the total of all the Debits and the total of all the Credits in the Trial Balance should be the same. That is, the Trial Balance should balance. Remember this does not mean that everything has been entered correctly. It just means that you have entered everything as a double entry.

If transactions are moved, changed or added after the first Trial Balance, these are normally called "Journal Adjustments", and shown separately in an accountants working papers.

An example of a Trial Balance
(using the transactions from Chapter 8):

	Trial Balance	
	Debit	Credit
Description	£	£
Sales		53000
Bank	53000	
Sales		5000
Debtors	5000	
Purchases	2000	
ABC Ltd (Creditors)		2000
Van	4000	
Bank		4000
Motor	2000	
Bank		2000
Bank Loan		1000
Bank	1000	
Total	67000	67000

...cont'd

You can see that for our:

- 6 transactions

- there are 12 entries

- so we have 6 double entries

You can see that we have the same total of Debits as Credits, i.e. £67,000.

> *You can put a transaction in the wrong category but as long as you make an entry in another category and one is a Debit and one a Credit, your accounts will still balance. They can be wrong but they will be balanced and be complete!*
>
> *Any errors should be picked up along the way or when looking at the accounts later i.e. figures higher or lower than they should be or categories you would expect missing altogether!*

Instead of every transaction being shown separately in the Trial Balance, transactions under the same categories are grouped together and just the **closing balance** is entered in the Trial Balance.

For example the Bank Category for the above transactions would look like this:

Category - Bank		
	Debit	**Credit**
Description	£	£
Sales	53000	
Van		4000
Motor		2000
Bank Loan	1000	
Closing Balance *		48000
Total	**54000**	**54000**

* Closing Balance = £53,000 + £1,000 - £4,000 - £2,000

Sales would look like this:

Category - Sales		
	Debit	Credit
Description	£	£
Bank		53000
Debtors		5000
Closing Balance	58000	
Total	58000	58000

And so the Trial Balance would look like this:

		Trial Balance	
		Debit	Credit
Description		£	£
Sales	(£53000 + £5000)		58000
Bank	(£53000 - £4000 - £2000 + £1000)	48000	
Debtors		5000	
Purchases		2000	
ABC Ltd (Creditors)			2000
Van		4000	
Motor		2000	
Bank Loan			1000
Total		61000	61000

Just the Closing Balances of **Bank** and **Sales** are included in the Trial Balance.

From Trial Balance to P & L and Balance Sheet

It is easy to produce a Proft & Loss (P & L) and Balance Sheet (BS) from a Trial Balance (TB). Just lay the P & L and Balance Sheet next to the Trial Balance and put the Trial Balance entries in their appropriate places in the P & L and BS.

If the Categories have just one entry, and it is say a Debit then it will be a Debit in the P & L or BS.

If the categories have more than one entry and they have been balanced off, then if the Closing Balance is say a Debit, it is entered in the Double Entry as a Credit:

Category - Sales		
	Debit	Credit
Description	£	£
Bank		53000
Debtors		5000
Closing Balance	58000	
Total	58000	58000

So the Closing Balance of £58,000 which is a Debit above, is entered in the Trial Balance as a Credit:

	Trial Balance	
	Debit	Credit
Description	£	£
Sales		58000

This is because the transactions in the Sales Category are actually Credits.

Category - Sales	Debit	Credit
	Debit	**Credit**
Description	£	£
Bank		53000
Debtors		5000
Closing Balance	58000	
Total	58000	58000

The £53,000 and £5,000 are Credits. They're balanced off with a Debit Closing Balance (£58,000) so both Debits and Credits total the same. Although the Closing Balance is a Debit, it goes into the Trial balance as a Credit.

But the simple way to remember it is: if you have a **Debit** closing balance on a Category, it will be entered in the Trial Balance as a **Credit** and vice versa.

Some Categories will have no balances and there is nothing more to do with them, i.e. they will not feature in the P & L or BS.

For example, IF the Debtors above had been paid during the year, this would be the position at the year end:

Category - Debtors	Debit	Credit
	Debit	**Credit**
Description	£	£
Sales	5000	
Bank		5000
Total	5000	5000

Category - Sales		
	Debit	Credit
Description	£	£
Debtors		5000
Closing Balance	5000	
Total	**5000**	**5000**

So you can see there is a closing balance for Sales but none for Debtors. We have totalled the Debits and Credits for Debtors and found they are the same so there is nothing owing or outstanding on either side and therefore there is no Debtors closing balance to go into the accounts.

Debtors have been cleared by being paid and no longer need to appear anywhere.

Note that the two entries had been Sales and Debtors but if the Debtors are paid, become Sales and Bank. In which case the Bank balance goes up by £5,000 and there are no Debtors.

BUT this was just for illustration purposes so you could see that sometimes there are no balances to take account of. However, in our accounts Debtors have not been paid so we still have Debtors of £5,000 to deal with.

We have started you off with Sales. See if you can put the remainder of the Trial Balance entries in the P & L and BS. The entries go in one OR the other.

Let us start by balancing off each and every Category. We will do all six for completeness. We have colour coded the double entry transactions. The Closing Balances are in **BOLD**

1. Sales of £53,000 made to Customers paid for by bank transfers, and

2. Sales of £5,000 on credit:

Category - Sales		
	Debit	**Credit**
Description	£	£
Bank		53000
Debtors		5000
Closing Balance	**58000**	
Total	**58000**	**58000**

The Double Entry for the Sales transactions of £53,000 is Bank – we have put the Bank Category at the end of the 6 transactions on p185.

The other Sales transaction of £5,000 is Debtors:

Category - Debtors		
	Debit	**Credit**
Description	£	£
Sales	5000	
Closing Balance		**5000**
Total	**5000**	**5000**

...cont'd

3 £2,000 stock (goods for you to sell) bought from a Supplier (ABC Ltd) on credit:

Category - Purchases		
	Debit	Credit
Description	£	£
ABC Ltd	2000	
Closing Balance		2000
Total	2000	2000

Category - Creditors (ABC Ltd)		
	Debit	Credit
Description	£	£
Purchases		2000
Closing Balance	2000	
Total	2000	2000

4 Van purchased with a cheque:

Category - Vehicles		
	Debit	Credit
Description	£	£
Bank (see p185)	4000	
Closing Balance		4000
Total	4000	4000

5 Vehicle expenses totalling £2,000 paid by bank debit card:

Category - Motor		
	Debit	Credit
Description	£	£
Bank (see below)	2000	
Closing Balance		2000
Total	2000	2000

6 Bank Loan of £1,000 by bank transfer:

Category - Bank Loan		
	Debit	Credit
Description	£	£
Bank (see below)		1000
Closing Balance	1000	
Total	1000	1000

Category - Bank		
	Debit	Credit
Description	£	£
Sales	53000	
Van		4000
Motor		2000
Bank Loan	1000	
Closing Balance		48000
Total	54000	54000

...cont'd

Now enter the Closing Balances in the Trial Balance. Remember if they are a Debit, enter them in the TB as a Credit, and if a Credit, as a Debit. We have done the first one, Sales.

Note: We have given you the totals at the bottom so after you have entered the TB figures, you can total up your figures and see if you are right:

	Trial Balance	
	Debit	Credit
	£	£
Sales		58000
Bank		
Debtors		
Purchases		
Creditors (ABC Ltd)		
Van		
Motor		
Bank Loan		
Total	61000	61000

Below is the TB you should have. The figure from the TB will go **either** in the P & L **or** the BS. Using the TB, we can now compile the P & L and BS.

If the figure in the TB is say a credit, it will be a credit in P & L or BS.

The full position is shown below:

	Trial Balance		P & L			BS	
	Debit	Credit	Expenses	Sales	Profit/ Loss	Assets	Liabilities
	£	£	£	£	£	£	£
Sales		58000		58000			
Bank	48000					48000	
Debtors	5000					5000	
Purchases	2000		2000				
Creditors (ABC Ltd)		2000					2000
Van	4000					4000	
Motor	2000		2000				
Bank Loan		1000					1000
			4000	58000	54000	→	54000
Total	61000	61000	B	A	(A - B)	57000	57000

...cont'd

The P & L and BS are above but will look more like this:

Profit & Loss	£	£
Sales		58000
Expenses		
Purchases	2000	
Motor	2000	4000
Profit		54000

Balance Sheet			
Assets		£	£
Fixed	Vehicles	4000	
Current	Bank	48000	
	Drs	5000	57000
Liabilities			
Creditors		2000	
Bank Loan		1000	3000
Net Assets			**54000**
Capital Account			
Plus Profit		54000	
Capital Account CF		**54000**	**54000**

So you have created a set of accounts from a Trial Balance!

Instead of showing each Category or Nominal as on p183 - 185, the business could just provide the information in a list:

	£
Sales (Bank)	53000
Debtors	5000
Purchases (Bank)	NIL
Creditors	2000
Vehicle purchased (Bank)	4000
Motor Expenses (Bank)	2000
Bank Loan received (Bank)	1000
Bank Balance`	48000

This would be very helpful to your accountant. But it is only one more step to the Trial Balance:

	Dr	Cr
	£	£
Sales (Bank)		53000
Sales (Debtors)		5000
Debtors	5000	
Purchases (Creditors)	2000	
Creditors		2000
Vehicle purchased (Bank)	4000	
Motor Expenses (Bank)	2000	
Bank Loan received (Bank)		1000
Bank Balance	48000	
	61000	61000

See the Trial Balance on p187.

Any transactions that are not 'cash' (i.e. cash or bank) will have two entries in the TB e.g. sales unpaid (debtors) are both **Sales** and **Debtors.**

Their Double Entry is therefore **Sales** and **Debtors**.

Similarly the Double Entry for Creditors is **Purchases** and **Creditors**.

Any transactions that are 'cash' will *seem* to only have one entry in the TB.

For example, sales paid into the bank of £53,000 *seem* to appear in the TB only once.

Where is the other Double Entry?

Of course, in the **Bank**. It is included in the bank balance of £48,000 (see Bank category on p185).

Nominals in a nutshell...

- The Categories we have been looking at, e.g. Sales, Bank, etc. are known in accountancy terms as "Nominals"

- All the transactions in each Category (or Nominal) are totalled for the year and "balanced off" with a Closing Balance

- Some Categories have no need of a Closing Balance, they are already balanced, and do not appear in the accounts, e.g. Debtors when they have been paid during the year

- The Closing Balances are entered in the Trial Balance (TB) as the opposite, e.g. a Debit Balance is entered as a Credit in the TB

- This is not as strange as it seems because the Closing Balance just represents all the transactions on the other side of the Category e.g. a Debit Closing balance represents Credits, so the entry we want in the TB is a Credit

- The TB must balance

- A Profit & Loss and Balance Sheet are produced from the TB

- You can even merely just list your "Cash" transactions and Debtors and Creditors and give these to your Accountant

- You can go one step further and prepare the Trial Balance

- Both should save you accountancy fees

- You could even prepare an initial P & L and BS!

We are now going to prepare the whole TB for our full Accounts above for Year 1 incorporating one or two of the other tricky Categories e.g. Depreciation.

Trial Balance that the Business Could Produce

If the business could produce an accurate Trial Balance of just "Cash" (i.e. cash and bank) transactions and debtors and creditors, the accounts would be half done.

Working with these transactions (in blue and green below) and one or two transactions that the accountant could have advised on during the year (in pink below), using Double Entry we are now going to produce the Trial Balance, AND Profit & Loss and Balance Sheet.

The business could do this and hand it to the accountant to finish the accounts.

> *Remember, if there is more than one transaction and a closing balance in the Category (or Nominal account), the entry in the Trial Balance is on the OPPOSITE side to the closing balance.*

Nominals & Trial Balance

KEY

BLUE = Bank   Black = Ordinary transactions
GREEN = Debtors/Creditors
PINK = As advised by accountant during the year

Sales of £53,500 to customers who paid into the bank
A sales refund of £500 made by bank transfer
Sales of £5,000 sold to customers on credit
Insurance recovery for lost sales £4,000

Hot tip

All bank transactions are
shown on p198 (in blue).

CATEGORIES OR NOMINALS				TRIAL BALANCE ENTRIES		
Sales						
Description	Debit	Credit			Debit	Credit
	£	£			£	£
Bank		53500				
Bank (Sales Refunds)	500					
Debtors		5000				
Bank (Insurance Recovery)		4000				
Balance	62000			Sales		62000
Total	62500	62500				

Debtors (Various)				TRIAL BALANCE ENTRIES		
	Debit	Credit			Debit	Credit
Description	£	£			£	£
Sales	5000					
Balance		5000		Debtors	5000	
Total	5000	5000				

a. The description indicates where the other entry is e.g. the £53,500 in Bank above is described as "Sales" which is where the corresponding entry is.
b. Every entry has a corresponding entry, i.e. every Debit has a Credit, e.g. in Sales, Debtors of £5,000 are a credit and are matched by a corresponding Debit in Debtors (various).
c. Three Nominal Accounts are involved in the Sales transactions – Sales, Debtors and Bank.

...cont'd

2 Purchases of £14,000 made and paid for Purchases of £2,000 made on credit

Purchases				TRIAL BALANCE ENTRIES		
Description	Debit	Credit			Debit	Credit
	£	£			£	£
Bank	14000					
Creditors	2000					
Balance		16000		Purchases	16000	
Total	16000	16000				

Creditors (Various)				TRIAL BALANCE ENTRIES		
Description	Debit	Credit			Debit	Credit
	£	£			£	£
Purchases		2000				
Balance	2000			Creditors		2000
Total	2000	2000				

3 Wages of £8,000 paid to employees
PAYE tax and national insurance of £500 owed at the year end
Grant of £1,000 received for employing apprentices

Wages				TRIAL BALANCE ENTRIES		
Description	Debit	Credit			Debit	Credit
	£	£			£	£
Bank	8000					
Grant		1000				
HMRC (Creditors)	500					
Balance		7500		**Wages**	7500	
Total	2500	2500				

HMRC				TRIAL BALANCE ENTRIES		
Description	Debit	Credit			Debit	Credit
	£	£			£	£
Wages		500				
Balance	500			HMRC		500
Total	500	500				

4 Rent for storage of £2,500 paid for 12 months in middle of year

Premises				TRIAL BALANCE ENTRIES		
Description	Debit	Credit			Debit	Credit
	£	£			£	£
Rent	2500					
Balance		2500		Premises	2500	
Total	2500	2500				

5 Repairs paid £500
Insurance Recovery £400

Repairs				TRIAL BALANCE ENTRIES		
Description	Debit	Credit			Debit	Credit
	£	£			£	£
Bank	500					
Insurance Recovery		400				
Balance		100		Repairs	100	
Total	500	500				

...cont'd

6 Various expenses paid:
Motor £2,000
Office £1,500
Advertising £2,000
Accountancy £500

Motor				TRIAL BALANCE ENTRIES		
Description	Debit	Credit			Debit	Credit
	£	£			£	£
Bank	2000					
Balance		2000		Motor	2000	
Total	2000	2000				

Office				TRIAL BALANCE ENTRIES		
Description	Debit	Credit			Debit	Credit
	£	£			£	£
Bank	1500					
Balance		1500		Office	1500	
Total	1500	1500				

Advertising				TRIAL BALANCE ENTRIES		
Description	Debit	Credit			Debit	Credit
	£	£			£	£
Bank	2000					
Balance		2000		Advertising	2000	
Total	2000	2000				

Accountancy				TRIAL BALANCE ENTRIES		
Description	Debit	Credit			Debit	Credit
	£	£			£	£
Bank	500					
Balance		500		Accountancy	500	
Total	500	500				

7 Vehicle purchased £4,000

Vehicles				TRIAL BALANCE ENTRIES		
Description	Debit	Credit			Debit	Credit
	£	£			£	£
Bank	4000					
Balance		4000		Vehicle	4000	
Total	4000	4000				

8 Bank transfer of £1,000 - Bank Loan

Bank Loan				TRIAL BALANCE ENTRIES		
Description	Debit	Credit			Debit	Credit
	£	£			£	£
Bank		1000				
Balance	1000			Bank Loan		1000
Total	1000	1000				

9 Owner takes £18,000 drawings during year

Drawings				TRIAL BALANCE ENTRIES		
Description	Debit	Credit			Debit	Credit
	£	£			£	£
Bank	18000					
Balance		18000		Drawings	18000	
Total	18000	18000				

...cont'd

Bank			TRIAL BALANCE ENTRIES	
Description	In (Debit) £	Out (Credit) £	Debit £	Credit £
Opening Balance	Nil			
Insurance Recovery (loss of sales)	4000			
Sales from Customers	53500			
Sales refunds		500		
Materials purchased		14000		
Wages		8000		
Grant - Wages	1000			
Premises		2500		
Repairs & Maintenance		500		
Insurance recovery for repairs	400			
Motor		2000		
Office or administration		1500		
Advertising		2000		
Accountancy		500		
Drawings		18000		
Capital introduced	0			
Vehicle purchased		4000		
Bank Loan	1000			
Closing Balance		6400	Bank 6400	
Total	59900	59900		

Here is the TB summarised, and then the P & L and BS compiled from the TB:

Trial Balance	Debit £	Credit £
Sales		62000
Debtors	5000	
Purchases	16000	
Creditors		2000
Wages	7500	
HMRC (Creditor)		500
Premises	2500	
Repairs	100	
Motor	2000	
Office	1500	
Advertising	2000	
Accountancy	500	
Vehicle	4000	
Bank Loan		1000
Drawings	18000	
Bank	6400	
Total	65500	65500

P & L	Expenses £	Sales £	Profit/ Loss £
Sales		62000	
Purchases	16000		
Wages	7500		
Premises	2500		
Repairs	100		
Motor	2000		
Office	1500		
Advertising	2000		
Accountancy	500		
	32100	62000	29900
	B	A	(A - B)

BS	Assets £	Liabilities £
Debtors	5000	
Creditors		2000
HMRC (Creditor)		500
Vehicle	4000	
Bank Loan		1000
Drawings	18000	
Bank	6400	
		29900
	33400	33400

So if you just list cash and bank transactions together with Debtors and Creditors at the year end and produce a Trial Balance, you will have done half of the job of preparing the accounts!

If you cannot manage a Trial Balance and just list cash and bank transactions, and debtors and creditors, you will have made a significant contribution to the preparation of the accounts.

Don't forget

"Cash" transactions are Cash AND Bank transactions.

...cont'd

You need to include bank transactions which do not appear on the bank statements until after the end of the year e.g. unpresented cheques, and should provide a reconciliation with the closing bank balance:

		£
31.3.10	Bank balance per bank statement	4000
30.3.10	Less Chq No 0021	100
31.3.10	Actual bank balance for Balance Sheet	3900

If you go on to the next section you will understand better why if you produce a TB with **just cash transactions and debtors & creditors at the year end**, you will have helped your accountant quite a lot. Minimising the time your accountant spends on your

accounts should mean lower accountancy bills.

You will also have a much better understanding of accounts.

But if you want an easy life, you could skip to VAT and Double Entry.

Trial Balance that the Accountant Produces

Finally we are going to look at what the accountant adds to the accounts and if you had prepared the TB above, what he adds to your TB. What he might do is check why accounts figures are different to the totals of each category that the business might have in their books.

For example, the accountant will deal with stock. The business just has to count stock and provide a list and total cost.

What else would the accountant deal with?

- The Electricity bill for £600 not issued until following year, the bill is for 3 months, 2 months of which are in our year

  So the accountant would include an Accrual in the accounts

- The Business rent of £2,500 for 12 months paid in middle of year, only 6 months of which relates to our year

  So the accountant would include a Prepayment in the accounts to move £1,250 (£2,500 x 6/12) into the following year

- The Repairs of £800 that might have to be paid for

  So the accountant is going to have to make a Provision

- The accountants bill for the accounts is going to be £600

  So the accountant will include another Accrual

- Debtors owing £350 are not going to pay

  So the accountant is going to write off the debt as bad

- The Van is going to depreciate with time

  The accountant needs to include depreciation in the accounts

- There is Stock and WIP

  The accountant needs to include them

The accountants adjustments are known as "Journals".

This is what your accountant will do to your TB. Remember every Debit has a Credit. For each of the transactions above, one double entry will affect the P & L and the other will affect the BS:

TRIAL BALANCE (FROM ABOVE)			ACCOUNTANTS JOURNALS			TB + JOURNALS	
	Debit	Credit		Debit	Credit	Debit	Credit
	£	£		£	£	£	£
Sales		62000					62000
Debtors	5000					5000	
Purchases	16000					16000	
Creditors		2000					2000
Wages	7500					7500	
HMRC (Creditor)		500					500
Premises	2500					2500	
			Premises (Prepayments)		1250		1250
			Premises (Accrual)	400		400	
			Accrual (BS)		400		400
			Prepayments (BS)	1250		1250	
Repairs	100					100	
			Repairs (Provision)	800		800	
			Provision (BS)		800		800
Motor	2000					2000	
Office	1500					1500	
Advertising	2000					2000	
Accountancy	500					500	
			Accountancy (Accrual)	600		600	
			Accrual (BS)		600		600
			Bad Debt	350		350	
			Debtors (BS)		350		350
Vehicle	4000					4000	
			Depreciation (P & L)	1000		1000	
			Depreciation (BS)		1000		1000
Bank Loan		1000					1000
Drawings	18000					18000	
			Closing Stock (BS)	1000		1000	
			(Stock) Purchases		1000		1000
			Closing WIP	2000		2000	
			Sales (WIP)		2000		2000
Bank	6400					6400	
Total	65500	65500		7400	7400	72900	72900

Notes: 1. Premises £2,500 dr + £400 dr – £1,250 cr = £1,650
2. Repairs £100 dr + £800 dr = £900
3. Accountancy £500dr + £600dr = £1,100

PROFIT & LOSS				BALANCE SHEET		
	Expenses	Sales	Profit/Loss		Assets	Liabilities
	£	£	£		£	£
Sales		62000				
				Debtors	5000	
Purchases	16000					
				Creditors		2000
Wages	7500					
				HMRC (Creditor)		500
Premises[1]	1650					
				Accruals (Premises)		400
				Prepayments	1250	
Repairs [2]	900					
				Provision (Repairs)		800
Motor	2000					
Office	1500					
Advertising	2000					
Accountancy [3]	1100					
				Accrual (Accountancy)		600
Bad Debt	350					
				Debtors		350
				Vehicle	4000	
Depreciation (P & L)	1000					
				Vehicle Depreciation		1000
				Bank Loan		1000
				Drawings	18000	
				Stock	1000	
Closing Stock		1000				
				WIP	2000	
Sales		2000				
				Bank	6400	
	34000	65000	31000			31000
	B	A	(A - B)		37650	37650

...cont'd

For every prepayment, accrual or provision, there will be two entries – one in the P & L and one in the BS.

This also applies to bad debts, depreciation, stock and WIP.

In a nutshell...

- The P & L and BS are now exactly the same as the accounts before we began Double Entry

- With Double Entry you have seen what you can do to produce a TB which will be useful to your accountant

- You have seen what your accountant does to get to a more advanced TB

- The TB gives everyone the security of knowing that everything is there because it balances!

- You have now seen the accounts for the first year come together, with and without Double Entry

Don't forget

We are explaining how accounts are put together to help your understanding. You need only list cash and bank transactions and debtors and creditors at the year end.

If you can list cash and bank transactions and debtors and creditors, it is only one small step to preparing a Trial Balance. If you do prepare the TB, it does not matter whether you are preparing the accounts for Year 1 or Year 10 because you will just be including the cash transactions and closing debtors and creditors of **your** year.

Now we are going on to look at Year 2.

Year 2 Double Entry and Trial Balance

Dealing with accounts for Year 2 and subsequent years is tricky so we have not put any VAT into the examples to make it easier.

First of all let us start with the bank.

Here is a summary of all the bank transactions in Year 2 as they might be shown on your bank statements:

Bank Statement	Payments	Deposits
	£	£
Sales		63000
Purchases	14000	
Wages	8500	
Premises	3100	
Repairs & Maintenance	900	
Motor	2000	
Office or Administration	1750	
Advertising	2000	
Accountancy	600	
Drawings	18000	
Bank Loan Repayments	400	
Loan Interest	100	
Closing balance	11650	

...cont'd

So you know now that these appear the opposite way round in Double Entry. So here is the bank Category or Nominal in the double entry records of the business:

Don't forget

You must include all bank transactions that you made in the year even if they do not all appear on the bank statements for the year e.g. a cheque you wrote which does not get cashed until the following year.

So you will have to include those transactions in your records too.

Bank

Description	Debits	Credits
	£	£
Sales	63000	
Purchases		14000
Wages		8500
Premises		3100
Repairs & Maintenance		900
Motor		2000
Office or Administration		1750
Advertising		2000
Accountancy		600
Drawings		18000
Bank Loan Repayments		400
Loan Interest		100
Closing balance		11650
Total	63000	63000

And here is the Trial Balance based **just on the bank transactions** showing Sales, Purchases, Wages etc.

We have not prepared each Nominal to save time but the Debits and Credits follow the Grid e.g. Sales are Credits and Expenses and Purchases are Debits:

Trial Balance – Year 2	Debit	Credit
	£	£
Sales - Bank		63000
Purchases - Bank	14000	
Wages - Bank	8500	
Premises - Bank	3100	
Repairs - Bank	900	
Motor - Bank	2000	
Office - Bank	1750	
Advertising - Bank	2000	
Accountancy- Bank	600	
Drawings - Bank	18000	
Loan Repayments - Bank	400	
Loan Interest - Bank	100	
Bank	11650	
Total	63000	63000

So for the Trial Balance, we have ended up back with the layout of the bank statements!

...cont'd

Let us add Debtors and Creditors (in green):

Trial Balance – Year 2	Debit	Credit
	£	£
Sales - Bank		63000
Sales - Debtors		6000
Closing Debtors	6000	
Purchases - Bank	14000	
Purchases - Creditors	4000	
Closing Creditors		4000
Wages - Bank	8500	
Wages - Creditors (HMRC)		600
HMRC	600	
Premises - Bank	3100	
Repairs - Bank	900	
Motor - Bank	2000	
Office - Bank	1750	
Advertising - Bank	2000	
Accountancy - Bank	600	
Loan Repayments - Bank	400	
Loan Interest - Bank	100	
Drawings - Bank	18000	
Bank	11650	
Total	73600	73600

So if you produced a Trial Balance as above, you would have done half the job of preparing the accounts.

But if you just gave your accountant a list of Categories (Nominals) and the total for each, and debtors and creditors, that would be good enough.

We now move to 'advanced' Double Entry bookkeeping. It is not essential that you understand everything completely. It will help though if you get the broad idea.

What we are going to do now is show you what the accountant would do to prepare the accounts from scratch i.e. if you had done nothing.

We are going to start with explaining how the **closing** balances from the previous year are dealt with.

These become the **opening** balances for our year, Year 2.

Hopefully, you are getting more familiar with Double Entry, and so we are going to stop saying "Categories" and just use the term Nominal Accounts or just 'Nominals'.

Remember we can forget last year's closing balances for the Nominals that went into the **P & L**. These were used in last year's **P & L**. That is the end of them.

However, the closing balances that went into last year's **BS** feature again in the following year's accounts. They're the opening balances of the following year, Year 2.

The balances brought forward for all the Nominals except Closing Stock (Stock BS) are used.

For example the Purchases Category or Nominal for Year 2 will start like this:

Creditors		
Description	Debit	Credit
	£	£
Balance BF		2000

The £2,000 was what was still owed to Suppliers at the end of Year 1.

You can see that the Creditors which were a Credit at the end of last year come forward and are a Credit to start the Creditors Nominal for the following year. One way of looking at it is that there was unfinished business from Year 1 and we must start Year 2 with it.

...cont'd

Then let us say that in Year 2 the business pays the outstanding Creditors and nothing else happens in Year 2. Creditors in Year 2 will finish the year like this:

Creditors		
Description	Debit	Credit
	£	£
Bal BF		2000
Bank	2000	
Total	2000	2000

There is no closing balance so there would be no Closing Creditors in the Balance Sheet of **Year 2**.

Stock starts the same way i.e. by bringing forward the closing balance from Year 1 to be the opening balance for Year 2:

Stock (BS)		
Description	Debit	Credit
	£	£
Balance BF	1000	

You can see that the stock Debit from the BS at the end of last year comes forward and is a Debit to start stock for the following year.

However, the special treatment for stock is that having brought forward the previous year balance, (opening stock for Year 2), we want to get rid of it and start again with closing stock. This is the only Nominal where this happens.

So for Year 2, the Double Entry treatment is to undo the stock from the previous year and start again.

We enter a Credit to match the Debit brought forward. It clears the Balance BF. We now have no Balance.

Stock (BS)		
Description	Debit	Credit
	£	£
Balance BF	1000	
Opening Stock (P & L)		1000
Total	1000	1000

The Double Entry for this is to put the same figure into the P & L. This is the Nominal that we are calling Stock (P & L):

Stock (P & L)		
Description	Debit	Credit
	£	£
Opening Stock (BS)	1000	
Closing Balance (Purchases)		1000
Total	1000	1000

This puts a Debit into the P & L described as **Opening Stock**. This increases Purchases. You will use this later.

Remember P & L Closing balances are "used up" in the P & L and not carried forward.

By making these two entries, we have got rid of last year's stock and can begin with a fresh sheet for Closing Stock of Year 2.

Now we are going to see at how this looks with a number of other Nominals.

Again, we have used the minimum number of Nominals so as not to overwhelm you - Sales, Debtors, Opening Stock, Closing Stock and Bank.

The method of clearing out last year's Stock (Opening Stock of Year 2) is shown on p213 in Step 5 in brown.

Year 2 Nominals & Trial Balance

1 Capital Account BF £13,000

Capital Account		
Description	Debit £	Credit £
Capital Account BF 1		13000
Balance	13000	
Total	13000	13000

TRIAL BALANCE		
	Debit £	Credit £
Capital A/c		13000

2 Sales of £63,000 made to various customers paid into the bank

3 Sales of £6,000 sold to customers on credit

Sales		
Description	Debit £	Credit £
Bank		63000
Closing Debtors		6000
Balance	69000	
Total	69000	69000

TRIAL BALANCE		
	Debit £	Credit £
Sales		69000

4 £4,650 paid into the bank from Opening Debtors

Various Debtors		
Description	Debit £	Credit £
Opening Drs	4650	
Bank		4650
Closing Debtors	6000	
Balance		6000
Total	10650	10650

TRIAL BALANCE		
	Debit £	Credit £
Cl/Debtors	6000	

5   Clear Opening Stock £1,000 from Balance Sheet

Opening Stock (BS)

Description	Debit	Credit
	£	£
Balance BF	1000	
Opening Stock to P & L		1000
Total	1000	1000

TRIAL BALANCE

	Debit	Credit
Note 2	£	£
Opening Stock BF	1000	
O/Stock P & L		1000

Opening Stock (P & L)

Description	Debit	Credit
	£	£
Opening Stock (BS)	1000	
Closing Balance (Purchases)		1000
Total	1000	1000

TRIAL BALANCE

	Debit	Credit
	£	£
Purchases	1000	

6   Include Closing Stock £2,000

Closing Stock (BS)

Description	Debit	Credit
	£	£
Closing Stock	2000	
Closing Balance		2000
Total	2000	2000

TRIAL BALANCE

	Debit	Credit
	£	£
Cl/Stock (BS)	2000	

Closing Stock (P & L)

Description	Debit	Credit
	£	£
Closing Stock (Purchases)		2000
Closing Balance	2000	
Total	2000	2000

TRIAL BALANCE

	Debit	Credit
	£	£
Cl/Stock (P & L)		2000

Remember closing stock appears in both P & L and BS.

...cont'd

(7) Bank

Bank			TRIAL BALANCE		
	Debit	Credit		Debit	Credit
	£	£		£	£
Opening balance[1]	7350				
Sales - from Customers	63000				
Sales - Opening Drs	4650				
Closing balance		75000	Bank	75000	
Total	75000	75000			
Total for 1-7				85000	85000

[1] *Capital Account BF and Bank Balance*

	£
Debtors	*4650*
Stock	*1000*
Bank	*7350*
Total Net Assets	*13000*
Capital Account BF	*13000*

To enable us to demonstrate using these few examples, we have made the bank opening balance £7,350 so we can work with the Capital Account BF of £13,000.

NB Everything must balance in the TB. It looks like there is no Double Entry for the closing debtors £6,000. The Double Entry is within the Sales of £69,000.
It looks like there is only one £1,000 relating to stock. The other Double Entry is represented by the Capital Account BF. The opening stock of £1,000 is one of the assets the Capital Account represents.

These are four examples of bringing forward balances from Year 1 – Capital Account, Debtors, Stock and Bank.

Note that there is never any brought forward (BF) balance for Sales. Their balances are always "used up" in the year and are never carried forward. Sales are a P & L item.

All the balances brought forward are used for Year 2, except Opening Stock.

So now we are able to have a go at the Trial Balance for Year 2.

We are going to break this up into stages and build it up into the finished product.

In the course of this, again we want you to appreciate what you can do to make things easier and quicker for your accountant. If it takes the accountant less time, this should be reflected in his bill.

As we go through we will make clear the stages that the accountant will deal with and the stages that you could deal with:

1. First, we start with what is effectively last year's Trial Balance (the closing balances of last year). This will have to be "brought forward" by the accountant into the accounts for this year and will be the "Opening Trial Balance" (the opening balances of our year, Year 2). You can leave this to the accountant

2. Next, we need to put together all the cash movements in the year so all the cash and bank transactions

   You can add to these the closing debtors and creditors.

   In our example, there are no cash transactions, just bank, so the next stage of the Trial balance is the "Trial Balance – Bank". This is the stage that you can provide

3. Then the Opening Trial Balance and the Year 2 Trial Balance can be combined – see the Year 2 Combined Trial Balance below. Your accountant can do that. We are just showing you how he does it with our Year 2 accounts

So you only need to do Step 2 above.

...cont'd

OPENING TRIAL BALANCE
(= closing trial balance of Year 1)

		Debit £	Credit £
Vehicle	4000		
Less Depreciation	1000	3000	
Debtors	5000		
Less Bad Debts	350	4650	
WIP		2000	
Stock		1000	
Creditors			2000
Wages Creditor (HMRC)			500
Prepmnts (Premises)		1250	
Accruals (Premises)			400
Provision (Repairs)			800
Accruals (Accntncy)			600
Bank Loan			1000
Capital Account			13000
Bank		6400	
Total		18300	18300

YEAR 2 TRIAL BALANCE
("Cash" movements and Debtors and Creditors of Year 2)

	Debit £	Credit £
Sales - Bank		63000
Sales - Debtors		6000
Closing Debtors	6000	
Purchases - Bank	14000	
Purchases - Creditors	4000	
Closing Creditors		4000
Wages - Bank	8500	
Wages - Creditor (HMRC)	600	
Wages		600
Premises - Bank	3100	
Repairs - Bank	900	
Motor - Bank	2000	
Office - Bank	1750	
Advertising - Bank	2000	
Accnty - Bank	600	
Loan Repments - Bank	400	
Loan Interest - Bank	100	
Drawings - Bank	18000	
Bank[1]	11650	
Total	73600	73600

[1] See Page 217

YEAR 2 FINAL TRIAL BALANCE

	Debit £	Credit £
Vehicle	3000	
Sales		58350
Sales - Debtors		6000
Closing Debtors	6000	
Opening WIP	2000	
Opening Stock	1000	
Purchases	12000	
Purchases - Creditors	4000	
Closing Creditors		4000
Wages	8000	
Wages-(Creditors HMRC)		600
Wages	600	
Opening Prepayments	1250	
Premises	2700	
Repairs	100	
Motor	2000	
Office	1750	
Advertising	2000	
Accountancy	0	
Bank Loan		1000
Loan Repayments	400	
Loan Interest	100	
Capital Account		13000
Drawings	18000	
Bank[2]	18050	
Total	82950	82950

[2] See Page 217

Bank

	Debit £	Credit £
Opening balance		
Sales	63000	
Purchases		14000
Wages		8500
Premises		3100
Repairs & Maintenance		900
Motor		2000
Office Administration		1750
Advertising		2000
Accountancy		600
Drawings		18000
Loan Repayments		400
Loan Interest		100
Closing balance[1]		11650
Total	63000	63000

Bank (including opening balance)

	Debit £	Credit £
Opening balance	6400	
Sales	63000	
Purchases		14000
Wages		8500
Premises		3100
Repairs & Maintenance		900
Motor		2000
Office Administration		1750
Advertising		2000
Accountancy		600
Drawings		18000
Loan Repayments		400
Loan Interest		100
Closing balance[2]		18050
Total	69400	69400

The Final Trial Balance combines the Opening Trial Balance and the Year 2 Trial Balance.

For example, sales received is £63,000 but some of this is money for Sales from the previous year i.e. Opening Debtors. Sales £63,000 less Opening Debtors £4,650 gives Sales for Year 2 of £58,350 – per the Final Trial Balance.

When preparing the acounts, the accountant will add on the Closing Debtors of £6,000 to produce Sales for Year 2 of £64,350 (£58,350 + £6,000).

So you can see that if you provide the cash movements and closing debtors and creditors, the accountant can work with them to build up the accounts.

...cont'd

The final stage is where the accountant makes any necessary adjustments or "journals". The final TB can then be produced:

YEAR 2 COMBINED TRIAL BALANCE	Debit	Credit	ACCOUNTANTS ADUSTMENTS OR "JOURNALS"	Debit	Credit
	£	£		£	£
Vehicle	3000				
			Vehicle Depreciation (BS)		750
			Vehicle Depreciation (P & L)	750	
Sales		58350			
Sales - Debtors		6000			
Closing Debtors	6000				
Opening WIP	2000		Cancel Opening WIP		2000
			Opening WIP (deducted from Sales)	2000	
			Closing WIP	**1000**	
			Closing WIP (Sales)		**1000**
Opening Stock	1000		Cancel Opening Stock		1000
			Opening Stock (added to Purchases)	1000	
			Closing Stock	2000	
			Closing Stock (Purchases)		2000
Purchases	12000				
Purchases - Creditors	4000				
Closing Creditors		4000			
Wages	8000				
Wages - Creditors (HMRC)		600			
Wages	600				
Premises Opening Prepayments	1250		**Opening Prepayments added to Premises**		**1250**
			Premises	**1250**	
			Closing Prepayments deducted from Premises		**1350**
			Closing prepayments	**1350**	
Premises	2700				
			Accruals - Premises - Electricity		**440**
			Accruals added to Premises	**440**	
Repairs	100				

FINAL TB		PROFIT & LOSS - YEAR 2				BALANCE SHEET - YEAR 2		
Debit	Credit		Expenses	Income	Profit		Assets	Liabilities
£	£		£	£	£		£	£
3000						Vehicle	3000	
	750					Depreciation		750
750		Depreciation	750					
	58350	Sales		58350[1]				
	6000	Sales		6000[1]				
6000						Debtors	6000	
	0							
2000		Opening WIP	2000[1]					
1000						WIP	1000	
	1000	Closing WIP		1000[1]				
	0							
1000		Opening Stock	1000[2]					
2000						Closing Stock	2000	
	2000	Closing Stock		2000[2]				
12000		Purchases	12000[2]					
4000		Purchases	4000[2]					
	4000					Creditors		4000
8000		Wages	8000[3]					
	600					Creditor (HMRC)		600
600		Wages	600[3]					
	0							
1250		Premises	1250[4]					
	1350	Prep Premises		1350[4]				
1350						Prepayments	1350	
2700		Premises	2700[4]					
	440					Accruals (Premises)		440
440		Premises	440[4]					
100		Repairs	100[4]					

219

YEAR 2 COMBINED TRIAL BALANCE	Debit	Credit	ACCOUNTANTS ADUSTMENTS OR "JOURNALS"	Debit	Credit
	£	£		£	£
Motor	2000				
Office	1750				
Advertising	2000				
Accountancy	0		Accrual (Accountancy)		620
			Accrual (Accountancy)	620	
Bank Loan		1000			
Loan Repayments	400	0			
Loan Interest	100	0			
Capital Account		13000			
Drawings	18000				
Bank	18050				
Total	82950	82950		10410	10410

So you can see that if you provide the cash movements and closing debtors and creditors, the accountant can do the rest. You will also need to provide him with a stock listing, and a sales listing for the year so he can check sales against the TB above.

FINAL TB		PROFIT & LOSS - YEAR 2				BALANCE SHEET - YEAR 2		
Debit	Credit		Expenses	Income	Profit		Assets	Liabilities
£	£		£	£	£		£	£
2000		Motor	2000					
1750		Office	1750					
2000		Advertising	2000					
	620					Accrual (Accntncy)		620
620		Accountancy	620					
	1000					Bank Loan		1000
400						Loan Repayments	400	
100		Loan Interest	100					
	13000					Capital Account		13000
18000						Drawings	18000	
18050						Bank	18050	
			39310	68700	29390			29390
89110	89110		B	A	(A - B)		49800	49800

Notes:

1. Sales are £63,350 (£58,350 + £6,000 + £1,000 – £2,000)

2. Purchases are £16,000 (£12,000 + £4,000)

3. Wages are £8,600 (£8,000 + £600)

4. Premises are £3,040 (£1,250 + £2,700 + £440 – £1,350)

5. The Capital Account for Year 2 is £24,390:

	£
Capital Account BF	13,000
Plus Profit	29,390
Less Drawings	18,000
Capital Account CF	24,390

The Profit & Loss you have created is the same P & L as on p150 in Chapter 7.

Summary

If you provide your accountant with the following, it should reduce your accountancy bill:

- Cash and bank transactions

- A list of the bank transactions that you have included in your figures but which do not appear on the bank statements until after the end of the year e.g. unpresented cheques and reconcile this with the closing bank balance

- A list of Debtors and Creditors

- Ideally a Trial Balance with all the above included

- Stock listing

- Sales listing

10 Double Entry for VAT

In Double Entry, VAT from each transaction is entered into one Nominal Account

Double Entries for VAT

To understand bookkeeping where VAT is involved, you have to pretend that the VAT on what you buy and what you sell is whisked away somewhere and dealt with separately, when the VAT Return is prepared and submitted.

The "somewhere" that the VAT goes is effectively an HMRC account and it works this way.

E.g. Goods of £1,200 incl VAT £200 are sold to Joseph Bloggs and he pays by internet transfer

This is what you are used to **if no VAT** is involved:

Sales		
Description	Debit	Credit
	£	£
Bank - Joseph Bloggs		1200

Bank		
Description	Debit	Credit
	£	£
Sales	1200	

However VAT is involved.

The VAT is whisked away to an HMRC (VAT) Category or Nominal so the sales figure excludes VAT:

Sales		
Description	Debit	Credit
	£	£
Bank		1000

and the VAT of £200 goes to:

HMRC (VAT)		
Description	Debit	Credit
	£	£
Sales or Output VAT		200

The bank still shows the figure including VAT because this was what was paid into the bank:

Bank		
Description	Debit	Credit
	£	£
Bank	1200	

So you have 3 Nominals instead of just 2 but everything balances. Sales of £1,000 + VAT of £200 = Bank £1,200.

Remember the VAT of £200 on Sales needs to be paid to HMRC.

So now let us say the VAT is entered on a VAT Return and paid.

HMRC (VAT)		
Description	Debit	Credit
	£	£
Sales or Output VAT		200
Bank	200	
Total	200	200

The HMRC (VAT) Category has no balance. It has been cleared.

Here is the bank. We have split the sales received of £1,200 into Sales £1,000 and VAT £200:

Bank		
Description	Debit	Credit
	£	£
Sales	1000	
VAT	200	
Payment to HMRC		200
Balance (money left in bank)		1000

Sales will be included in the accounts at £1,000 (£1,200 less VAT of £200) because the accounts figures are exclusive of VAT i.e. without VAT.

You can see that after paying the VAT, the business has £1,000 in the bank which is the sales without VAT. The VAT never belongs to the business – it is HMRC's.

Now we are going to assume that our business is VAT registered and bring in VAT. However so as not to overload you, we are going to assume that there is VAT on Sales but none of the Expenses except Purchases have VAT.

This is unlikely but it means we can look at VAT on just Sales and Purchases and make it easier to understand.

We are now going to treat the £62,000 Sales and £16,000 Purchases as including VAT.

In other words they are the value of goods or services plus VAT of 20%.

So Sales are actually £51,667 plus VAT of 20% £10,333 to give a total of £62,000 (£51,667 + £10,333).

Purchases are £13,333 plus 20% £2,667 to give the total of £16,000 (£13,333 + £2,667).

We call the figure excluding VAT the "Net" figure. We call the figure including VAT the "Gross" figure.

You can work out the **Net** figure by taking the Gross and dividing it by 1.2 (VAT rate 20%) so Gross £1,200 divided by 1.2 is £1,000, which is the Net figure excluding VAT

You can work out the **VAT** by taking the Gross and dividing it by 6 (VAT rate 20%) so Gross £1,200 divided by 6 is £200, which is the VAT.

Remember you have a choice how you calculate VAT. VAT can be accounted for on everything whether it has been paid or not ("Accruals" VAT) or just on what has been paid ("Cash Accounting" VAT).

So if the business was on Cash Accounting VAT it would only pay VAT on sales received and not on debtors and could only claim VAT on purchases paid, not on creditors.

We are going to use the accounts for Year 1 to demonstrate VAT. In Year 1 there were total sales for VAT of £58,000 of which £53,500 were received, £500 refunded and £5,000 were owed. (We can ignore the insurance proceeds of £4,000 because there is no VAT for insurance proceeds):

Sales		
Description	Debit	Credit
	£	£
Bank		53500
Bank (sales refunds)	500	
Debtors		5000
Balance	58000	
Total	58500	58500

We have £14,000 Purchases paid and Creditors of £2,000.

As we are now treating the business as VAT registered, those

Beware

Very big businesses must pay VAT on the Accruals basis.

Don't forget

Most businesses pay VAT on Cash Accounting because it saves them paying VAT on their sales before they have received them.

...cont'd

figures are "Gross" i.e. include VAT.

Let us be clear about the Gross, Net and VAT. We need to include every transaction so the Sales refund £500 as well as the Sales of £53,500.

We have split the Sales and Purchase into paid and not paid so we can calculate the VAT to be paid if VAT is paid on Cash Accounting.

Here are all the figures we will be working with

Blue = Bank or actual payments

		A Gross £	B Net £	A - B VAT £
Sales received	53500	Divide by 1.2 =	44583	8917
Sales refund	500	Divide by 1.2 =	417	83
Sales owed	5000	Divide by 1.2 =	4167	833
Purchases paid	14000	Divide by 1.2 =	11667	2333
Purchases owed	2000	Divide by 1.2 =	1667	333

We are going to deal with them one by one. We will start with the accounts figures and then split the VAT off in stages.

Firstly Sales received without the VAT shown separately:

Sales		
Description	Debit	Credit
	£	£
Bank		53500

Bank		
Description	Debit	Credit
	£	£
Sales	53500	

Then the Sales without VAT:

Sales		
Description	Debit	Credit
	£	£
Bank		44583

With the VAT shown separately in its VAT Category or Nominal:

HMRC (VAT)		
Description	Debit	Credit
	£	£
Sales or Output VAT		8917

The Bank is the same. £53,500 has still been banked but we have split the £53,500 into sales and sales VAT:

Bank		
Description	Debit	Credit
	£	£
Sales	44583	
Sales or Output VAT	8917	
TOTAL	53500	

Then let us introduce the Sales Refund of £500.

Here are the Sales refunds net of VAT (£500 ÷ 1.2 = £417):

Sales		
Description	Debit	Credit
	£	£
Bank (Sales Refunds)	417	

Here is the VAT (£500 ÷ 6 = £83):

HMRC (VAT)		
Description	Debit	Credit
	£	£
Sales	83	

Putting them all together:

Sales		
Description	Debit	Credit
	£	£
Bank		44583
Bank (Sales Refunds)	417	

HMRC (VAT)		
Description	Debit	Credit
	£	£
Sales		8917
Refunds	83	

The bank is still:

Bank		
Description	Debit	Credit
	£	£
Sales	44583	
Sales VAT	8917	
Sales refunds		417
Sales refunds VAT		83
TOTAL	53500	500

Then let us include the Debtors (£5,000 ÷ 1.2 = £4167):

Sales		
Description	Debit	Credit
	£	£
Debtors		4167

Debtors		
Description	Debit	Credit
	£	£
Sales	4167	
HMRC(VAT)	833	

Notice the total in Debtors is £5,000 (£4,167 + £833) because this is what will be paid eventually and will clear debtors. The Double Entry when the £5,000 is paid will of course be **Bank**.

The VAT Category or Nominal will look like this:

HMRC (VAT)		
Description	Debit	Credit
	£	£
Sales or Output VAT		833

...cont'd

The full HMRC (VAT) Nominal will be:

HMRC (VAT)		
Description	Debit	Credit
	£	£
Sales		8917
Refunds	83	
Debtors		833

Next, we will deal with the VAT on Purchases paid:

Purchases		
Description	Debit	Credit
	£	£
Bank	11667	

HMRC (VAT)		
Description	Debit	Credit
	£	£
Creditors	2333	

Next we will deal with the VAT on Purchases owed (creditors):

Purchases		
Description	Debit	Credit
	£	£
Creditors	1667	

Creditors		
Description	Debit	Credit
	£	£
Purchases		1667
Purchase or Input VAT		333

HMRC (VAT)		
Description	Debit	Credit
	£	£
Purchase or Input VAT	333	

The full HMRC (VAT) Nominal will now be:

HMRC (VAT)		
Description	Debit	Credit
	£	£
Sales received		8917
Refunds	83	
Sales owed		833
Purchases paid	2333	
Purchases owed	333	
Balance	7000	
Total	9750	9750

The balance of £7,000 is the VAT owed to HMRC on an Accruals basis. If it was paid to HMRC it would clear the VAT Nominal and the bank balance would go down by £7,000.

But we will work on the basis that it was not paid and is still owed.

Now let us include everything in a TB, Profit & Loss and Balance Sheet.

Nominals and TB with VAT

KEY

Blue = Bank   Black = Ordinary transactions

Pink = As advised by accountant during the year

1 Sales of £53,500 to various customers paid into the bank
A sales refund of £500 made by internet bank transfer
Sales of £5,000 sold to customers on credit
Insurance recovery for lost sales £4,000

Sales			TRIAL BALANCE ENTRIES	
Description	Debit	Credit	Debit	Credit
	£	£	£	£
Bank		44583		
Bank Refunds	417			
Debtors		4167		
Bank (Insurance)		4000		
Balance	52333		Sales	52333
Total	52750	52750		

Debtors (Various)				
Description	Debit	Credit		
	£	£		
Sales	4167			
VAT	833			
Balance		5000	Debtors	5000
Total	5000	5000		

2 Purchases of £14,000 made and paid for
Purchases of £2,000 made on credit

Purchases			TRIAL BALANCE ENTRIES	
Description	Debit	Credit	Debit	Credit
	£	£	£	£
Bank	11667			
Creditors	1667			
Balance		13334	Purchases	13334
Total	13334	13334		

Creditors (Various)				
Description	Debit	Credit		
	£	£		
Purchases		1667		
VAT		333		
Balance	2000		Creditors	2000
Total	2000	2000		

VAT

Description	Debit £	Credit £
Sales received		8917
Sales refunds	83	
Debtors		833
Purchases paid	2333	
Creditors		333
Balance	7001	
Total	9750	9750

TRIAL BALANCE ENTRIES

	Debit £	Credit £
VAT		7001

Bank

	In £	Out £
Opening balance	Nil	
Sales - Insurance	4000	
Sales	44583	
Sales VAT	8917	
Sales refunds		417
Sales refunds-VAT		83
Purchases		11667
Purchase VAT		2333
Closing balance		43000
Total	57500	57500

TRIAL BALANCE ENTRIES

	Debit £	Credit £
Bank	43000	

TRIAL BALANCE

	Debit £	Credit £
Sales		52333
Debtors	5000	
Purchases	13334	
Creditors		2000
VAT		7001
Bank	43000	
Total	61334	61334

PROFIT AND LOSS

			Profit £
Sales		52333	
Purchases	13334		
	13334	52333	38999
	B	A	(A - B)

BALANCE SHEET

	Assets £	Liabilities £
Debtors	5000	
Creditors		2000
VAT		7001
Bank	43000	
		38999
	48000	48000

Note the figures are slightly different to the ones we have looked at because of the effect of rounding several figures to whole numbers

...cont'd

The £7,000 VAT appears in the Balance Sheet as a Creditor along with the Creditors for Purchases of £2,000, but the VAT creditor will be shown separately. Note that Purchases Creditors in the BS include VAT (see Step 2 on page 234).

Remember we have restricted these examples to sales and purchases only so the P & L and BS are very simple – they do not include any of the other items from our accounts.

The VAT payable on Cash Accounting would not be £7,000 though. It would be £6,500:

CASH ACCOUNTING		
VAT		
Description	Debit	Credit
	£	£
Sales received		8917
Refunds	83	
Purchases paid	2333	
Balance	6500	
Total	8917	8917

This because the business is not having to pay VAT on its Debtors (although it cannot also claim VAT on its Creditors).

Compare this to the position in the TB above i.e. Accruals:

ACCRUALS		
VAT		
Description	Debit	Credit
	£	£
Sales received		8917
Refunds	83	
Debtors		833
Purchases paid	2333	
Creditors	333	
Balance	7000	
Total	9750	9750

Starting with £7,000 and taking off the VAT on Sales owed and adding back the VAT on Purchases owed you can see how we get to £6,500 using Cash Accounting.

	£
VAT Payable Accruals	7000
Less VAT on Debtors	833
	6167
Plus VAT on Creditors	333
Total VAT Cash Accounting	6500

Paying tax on Cash Accounting means that the VAT is out of line with the VAT Creditor in the Balance Sheet. The VAT creditor per the BS is the VAT owed on Accruals. The VAT actually owed at the BS date is what is owed on Cash Accounting. They are rarely the same.

So if the business is on Cash Accounting, until the business ceases the VAT creditor in the BS will not be the same as the VAT actually owed at the BS date.

This does not matter because it will catch up when the business ceases. In the last year of the business payments from all Debtors will be received and all the Creditors will be paid, and the VAT paid over to HMRC, clearing everything and bringing it into line.

The explanations above are merely to show to you how VAT affects the preparation of accounts.

We have said that if you provide your accountant with the following, it should reduce your accountancy bill:

- Cash and bank transactions

- A list of the bank transactions that you have included in your figures but which do not appear on the bank statements until after the end of the year e.g. unpresented cheques

- A list of Debtors and Creditors

- Ideally a Trial Balance with all the above included

- Stock listing

- Sales listing

If you are VAT registered and you have completed VAT Returns and you have not kept full double entry records, he will also need your VAT listings so he can see what VAT needs to be deducted from each category of expenses and from sales, so that the figures in the accounts (in the P & L) exclude VAT.

So if you are VAT registered, your record of cash and bank transactions must show the VAT and the amount excluding VAT **separately.**

If you have kept a proper Cashbook you have split off the VAT in the records and have the Net figures in the Expenses columns. This will be your listing. He will be able to work from this:

Bill Ref	Invoice Date	Invoice Paid Date	Cheque No	Supplier	Total (Net + VAT)	Purchase VAT	Net Expenses	
							Purchases	Employee
					£	£	£	£
1/2/3		15/5/12	010	ABC Ltd	120.00	20.00	100.00	

This record shows the 'cash' (cash and bank) transaction with VAT separately. This is what is needed if you are VAT registered.

If you have filed your own VAT Returns, your accountant will need copies of the VAT Returns.

Summary

- In Double Entry, the VAT part of a payment is put in its own HMRC (VAT) account, leaving the Net figures to be included in the accounts

- You can calculate the Net figure by taking the Gross figure (what is actually paid) and dividing it by 1.2 (VAT rate 20%)

- You can calculate the VAT from the Gross figure by dividing by 6 (VAT rate 20%)

- It does not matter to Double Entry whether you are paying VAT on Accruals or Cash Accounting, the accounts will be prepared on an accruals basis using the Net figures

- The VAT Creditor in the BS will rarely be the VAT actually owed at the BS date if the business is on Cash Accounting

- The accountant will need your Cashbook or VAT listings and VAT returns if you do not keep Double Entry records

11 Accounting Software

Accounting software can help reduce the burden of bookkeeping

Software Packages

Sage

Sage is probably the most used accounting software system. It gets you to enter transactions into various sections of the software. You enter bank transactions and invoices in different places and then match them up on the same screen.

You can produce a Trial Balance and even a P & L and BS from your entries but a lot of bookkeepers and businesses just hand over what they have done and the accountant uses the information to produce accounts.

Sage is sometimes not used by businesses as it was intended.

Others

There are other standard software packages on the market. All the software works much the same way i.e. there is a place to enter invoices and a place to enter bank and cash transactions.

You may find Sage and other software just process the standard transactions, you and your accountant have to make adjustments manually.

The adjustments made to the accounts by the accountant for one year are not automatically included in the software data for the following year. So the P & L and BS produced by the software at the year end are often inaccurate because the accounts did not start from the right position. Therefore, accountants often just use the basic data from the software, and possibly the Trial Balance. Then, produce the P & L and BS themselves. To keep the figures accurate on the system, manual journal entries need to be made to reflect the adjustments made by the accountnat.

One reason why businesses use an accountancy software package is to maintain a database of customers and suppliers.

The software usually enables them to generate invoices and reminders easily, and may also provide useful standard letters to customers/suppliers. This is obviously not the main purpose of the software. However, it does take care of Double Entry bookkeeping, provides an adequate method of recording day-to-day transactions and enables a basic Trial Balance to be produced.

Hot tip

Series of In Easy Steps guides are available to help you use Sage. Visit *www.ineasysteps.com* to see the full range and choose the one that covers your version of Sage. An excerpt from Sage 50 Accounts 2012 in easy steps is included on pages 282-283 to get you started.

Spreadsheet Solutions

Spreadsheets

Commonly businesses make listing of sales invoices and invoices for business expenses on spreadsheets but rarely enter sufficient information to enable them to be matched with bank transactions.

Or they produce wonderful but complicated spreadsheets with everything cross-referenced but not so it is easy to see, and not with bank transactions listed so they are easy to check against the bank statements.

The key is to use as few spreadsheets as possible and make them do as much work as possible.

There are various simple spreadsheets on the market e.g. Bright Bookkeeping, DIY accounting, Mr Spreadsheet, etc.

Find one that you like and is easy to use especially if it produces a TB for your accountant, and use it.

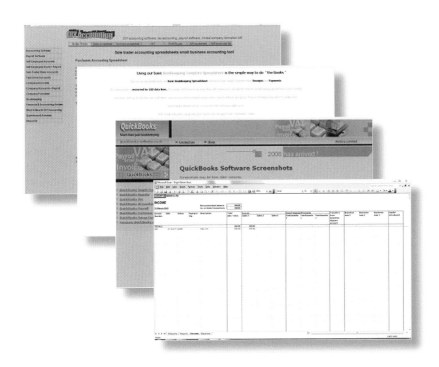

Summary

- Accountancy software may appear to be complicated to use, and often the data entered will need to be reviewed to produce the final accounts

- Standard accountancy software generally allows the business to generate invoices and letters to the customers and suppliers, especially when the business has a large customer base and/or generates a large number of invoices

- Standard accountancy packages also offer a stock management system, which is also useful

- Spreadsheets can be flexible and more useful if they are simple and produce a Trial Balance for your accountant

- Understanding the basic principles of accounting and the records you need to keep helps you to choose an accountancy software or spreadsheet solution that suits your business. Some of the options are listed in this chapter for your consideration

12 Other Financial Statements

Financial statements can be an invaluable source of information for business

Management Accounts

Why are they needed?

Management accounts can help you see how things are going as you go along. If there is a problem, you will then have a chance to sort it out before it does too much damage to the business. Similarly if some part of the business is doing well you will be able to see this early and may be able to expand it and do even better.

Different businesses will produce management accounts for different parts of the business, depending on what is important to them. These could include:

- The sales process - such as pricing, distribution and debtors

- The purchasing process - such as pricing, stock records and creditors

- Fixed assets - including identification numbers, cost and date of purchase, etc

- Employees

Businesses may want management accounts to show information for each sales outlet or factory or office so the performance of each can be measured. There may also be information, for example, to show how well a particular product has done in different shops.

For businesses selling more than one product, it is advisable to know what each costs, what it is sold for, what profit is made on it and what total profit is made from all the sales of that product. This should allow you to see if profitable products are subsidising others and take action i.e. you can stop selling the less profitable product!

There is no legal requirement to prepare management accounts, but it is hard to run a sizeable business effectively without them. Most sizeable companies produce them regularly e.g. monthly or quarterly.

Management accounts analyse the past and may make projections or forecasts about the future e.g. on sales, cash, cashflow and profit. Future management accounts can measure the forecasts against what has actually happened and allow the business to improve future forecasts.

Management accounts give you more control over the business e.g. they enable you to control cash, stocks, expenses, gross profit, overall profitability, etc for the whole business and for parts of the business.

Banks and other lenders may ask for management accounts when looking at lending.

Cashflow Forecasts

We produced a cashflow **statement** in Chapter 5 when we turned a Balance Sheet produced on an accruals basis into a statement of cash transactions.

A cashflow **forecast** is different from a cashflow statement:

● A cashflow forecast is used to predict expected rises and falls in cash over the coming year or other period

● A cashflow statement is a statement of cash movements that have already happened. A cashflow forecast is a prediction of future cash movements

We'll look at Cashflow Forecast for Year 1 of our business.

But here is a reminder of the bank position:

Bank Nominal		
	In	Out
	£	£
Money at beginning or opening balance	Nil	
Sales - Insurance recovery	4000	
Sales - from Customers	53500	
Sales refunds		500
Materials Purchased (£16000 less Suppliers not paid, £2000)		14000
Wages		8000
Grant - Wages	1000	
Premises		2500
Repairs & Maintenance		500
Repairs (Insurance Recovery)	400	
Motor		2000
Office or Administration		1500
Advertising		2000
Accountancy		500
Drawings		18000
Vehicle purchased		4000
Bank Loan	1000	
Bank balance at end or closing balance		6400
Total	59900	59900

...cont'd

Cashflow Forecast for Year 1 of our business:
Note: The total column on the far right matches the Bank nominal transactions.

Monthly Cash Flow Projection													
Luxury Windows Ltd													
Y/e 31st Mar 2013													
	Month 1	Month 2	Month 3	Month 4	Month 5	Month 6	Month 7	Month 8	Month 9	Month 10	Month 11	Mth 12	Total
	£	£	£	£	£	£	£	£	£	£	£	£	£
CASH ON HAND (begin. of month) A	0	2350	2800	7000	5900	8450	6650	6000	5050	3150	4200	4400	0
CASH RECEIVED													
Sales (net of refunds)	4000	5000	4000	3500	6000	5500	4500	3000	5000	4000	3000	5500	53000
Insurance Recoveries/Grants	0	4000	1000			400							5400
Loans/Capital Introduced	0								1000				1000
TOTAL CASH RECEIVED B	4000	5000	8000	4500	6000	5500	4900	3000	6000	4000	3000	5500	59400
TOTAL CASH AVAILABLE A+B	4000	7350	10800	11500	11900	13950	11550	9000	10050	7150	7200	9900	59400
CASH PAID OUT													
Purchases	0	2000	1000	2000	1000	1500	2500	1000	1500	500	500	500	14000
Employees Salaries & Wages	0	700	700	700	700	700	700	700	700	700	700	1000	8000
Business premises	0					2500							2500
Repairs and maintenance	0		100	200			200						500
Administration	150	150	150	150	150	150	150	150	150	150	0	0	1500
Insurance													
Advertising	0			1000		500		500					2000
Motor Vehicles	0	200	100	50	100	200	500	100	50	100	100	500	2000
Staff Travel & Meals													
Professional Services			250			250							500
Finance Interest & Charges													
Miscellaneous Costs													
Bad debts													
Purchase of Assets									4000				4000
Loan Repayments													
Drawings	1500	1500	1500	1500	1500	1500	1500	1500	1500	1500	1500	1500	18000
TOTAL CASH PAID OUT C	1650	4550	3800	5600	3450	7300	5550	3950	7900	2950	2800	3500	53000
CASH POSITION (End of month) A+B–C	2350	2800	7000	5900	8450	6650	6000	5050	3150	4200	4400	6400	6400

Note: Sales are shown net of refunds i.e. £53,500 – £500 = £53,000

The forecast opposite shows you months when cash is low e.g. Month 9. If the cash position for any of the months was a Minus, the business would come to a stop unless it could bring in money e.g. from debtors earlier than expected, delay paying creditors or get an overdraft.

Banks are very keen on cashflow forecasts especially when considering overdraft facilities e.g. for business growth.

Summary

- There are various types of financial statements. Annual accounts, management accounts, cashflow statements and forecasts

- Management accounts for bigger businesses give the businesses more control e.g. over sales and expenses (especially purchases) both for the whole business and/or parts of it

- Cashflow **statements** are a statement of a past cash position. They show where money came from and where it went

- Cashflow **forecasts** are a prediction of the future cash position. They enable the business to spot months when cash may be tight and take action to ensure a more even cashflow

- Banks often ask for management accounts and/or cashflow forecasts when businesses apply for loans or overdrafts

13 Business Tax

Falling foul of HMRC can give businesses a very large and unexpected bill

Profit for Tax Purposes

Adjustments required to arrive at profit for tax

Profit for tax is often different from the profit in the accounts.

The accounts profit figure is the starting point for the figure that is going to be used for calculating tax due, provided the accounts have been prepared using Generally Accepted Accounting Practice (GAAP).

Tax law specifies that depreciation on equipment, motor vehicles, etc. should be allowed as Capital Allowances in accordance with the Capital Allowance rules. This is covered further on page 256.

So the first adjustment to make to profit figure in the accounts is to add back the depreciation, in other words to make the profit figure as though depreciation had never been claimed in the P & L. Then, deduct Capital Allowances (HMRC's version of depreciation) in accordance with Capital Allowances rules.

So add back depreciation and deduct Capital Allowances from the Profit figure in the accounts to arrive at a different figure of Profit for tax.

	£
Profit per accounts	31000
Plus Depreciation	1000
Total	32000
Less Capital Allowances	4000
Profit for tax	28000

There is one exception to adding back depreciation. For **companies,** depreciation on goodwill is allowable for tax provided it is calculated in accordance with accountancy principles (and the goodwill was created after 31.03.02), so you do not need to add that back.

Other adjustments may be due to the profit per the accounts, the most common of which is probably Entertainment. While many businesses wine and dine their customers and suppliers to some extent or another and include entertainment as a legitimate expenses in their accounts, tax law does not allow entertainment expenses for tax purposes and they have to be added back to the accounts profit figure.

Note:Tax in the company accounts example has been worked out on the profit according to the accounts to keep things simple (i.e. without any tax adjustments).

Capital Allowances

Capital Allowances from tax are generally permitted for the same items that are depreciated in the accounts, e.g. vehicles, equipment, office furniture. (HMRC tend to call equipment and office furniture Plant & Machinery (P & M)). Claiming Capital Allowance on P & M can be complicated and beyond the scope of this book.

Depreciation and Capital Allowance (CAs) are not the same. For example, many accounts allow depreciation of 25% on a reducing balance on equipment, and HMRC currently generally allow 100%. However, that is not the only difference and you will almost certainly need accountancy help or training to correctly calculate CAs which change frequently. One of the reasons for the changes is successive governments have followed a policy of giving higher CAs to "greener" vehicles, for example.

There may be an entry for Deferred Taxation in accounts. This is commonly an adjustment to reflect the fact that the tax relief for capital allowances is generous for the year assets are purchased but the tax relief may need to be clawed back when the assets are sold, and so there is a tax bill waiting in the future.

Tax Deadlines & Penalties

Sole traders

Sole traders and partnerships have to include their accounts figures on self assessment Tax Returns and file these by 31st January following the end of the tax year at latest.

A tax year is 6th April to 5th April in the UK, so the tax year 2012/13 is 6.4.12 to 5.4.13, and the Tax Return for this year (Yr 2012/13) needs to be filed by 31st January 2014.

There are penalties for failing to submit self assessment Tax Returns in time and these get stiffer and increase the later the Tax Return is filed.

The first penalty is £100. Then if the Tax Return has still not been submitted 3 months after the deadline (by 30th April), there are further penalties of £10 per day for up to 90 days so £900!

If the Tax Return has still not been submitted 6 months after the deadline (by 31st July), there is another penalty of £300 or 5% of the tax due whichever is higher. If the Tax Return is 12 months late (i.e. still outstanding at the following 31st January) another £300 penalty or 5% of the tax is due, or even 100% of the tax due in serious cases!

Some Tax Returns cannot be filed online and have to be submitted in paper form by an earlier deadline of 31st October.

Companies

Companies have to file a company Tax Return within 12 months after the company year finishes. The tax a company pays is called Corporation Tax (CT). The company has to send its accounts and a computation of how it has arrived at its profit for tax with the Corporation Tax Return.

However, the company has to pay its Corporation Tax 9 months after the end of its year. So this tends to force accounts to be prepared within 9 months of the year end so that the tax can be calculated. If the accounts have not been prepared by the time the tax is due to be paid, then an estimate of the tax should be paid.

There are penalties for failing to submit the CT Return in time.

Beware

Penalties will be charged even if when the return is eventually submitted there is no tax to pay!

...cont'd

You must file your VAT return AND pay the VAT due if you want to avoid surcharges. Just filing the return and paying the VAT later will count as a late return.

Beware

We have seen instances when HMRC's letter does not arrive and the first notification you get may be a surcharge notice after two or more late VAT returns.

258

These are presently £100 and then another £100 if the Return is another 3 months late. (If the Company has been late 3 years running these £100 penalties rise to £500.)

In addition to these penalties, if the CT Return is more than 18 months late, HMRC will charge further penalties. If the CT Return is submitted 18 - 24 months after the end of the company's year, the penalty is 10% of any unpaid CT; if more than 24 months late, another 10%.

VAT Returns

VAT Returns usually cover 3 months and have to be filed by the end of the 4th month. E.g. a VAT Return for the 3 months or a quarter end 30.6.13 would have to be filed by 31.7.13.

There are penalties or surcharges for late VAT Returns. Surcharges can be 2%, 5%, 10% and 15% of the VAT due depending on how many VAT returns have been late in a row. HMRC say they write and warn businesses after one VAT Return is late and only impose a surcharge for future VAT returns submitted late.

Checks of Tax Returns

If HMRC check Tax Returns and find them to be wrong and more tax is due, they will charge a penalty unless "reasonable care" was taken to get the tax right. It is very difficult to persuade HMRC that reasonable care has been taken. Ignorance of the law is no excuse.

The penalty is a percentage of the extra tax due when HMRC corrects your mistake.

If the business draws the mistake to the attention of HMRC before HMRC notice it, then penalties are "unprompted". If HMRC find the mistake first or suspect it and begin asking questions about it, then the penalties are "Prompted".

There are different penalty ranges for "Unprompted" and "Prompted" errors.

Penalty ranges for unprompted and prompted disclosure

Type of error	Penalty range for unprompted disclosure	Penalty range for prompted disclosure
Careless	0% - 30%	15% - 30%
Deliberate but not concealed	20% - 70%	35% - 70%
Deliberate and concealed	30% - 100%	50% - 100%

So a deliberate error not concealed which the business tells HMRC about before HMRC ask any questions would be liable to a penalty of 20% - 70% of the extra tax, and a deliberate error that HMRC discovered would be in the penalty range 35% - 70%.

A deliberate **and** concealed error that HMRC find themselves would give a penalty of 50% - 100%!

Remember, these percentages are applied to the extra tax that is found to be due. So if the penalty percentage was, say 30% and the extra tax due was, say £5,000, you would have to pay:

	£
Tax due	5000
Penalty £5000 @ 30%	1500
Total	6500

HMRC would also charge interest on the tax of £5,000 from the date it ought to have been paid!

Don't forget

These time limits and rates are valid at the time of going to print. It's advisable to check the prevailing rates with your local tax office.

Summary

- A business will have more chance of being successful if it has good records and reliable up-to-date accounts

- It should be able to avoid unnecessary costs like late filing penalties and bills for extra tax if it uses an accountant

We have covered a lot of ground in this book but hope that you have found its contents helpful.

At the end of this book there is a set of questions you can use if you wish to see what you have found out.

NEWS

HMRC are considering allowing small businesses to prepare accounts on a cash basis as for VAT. There would be a turnover limit. Businesses below this limit would be able to use the cash basis. HMRC are also looking at other methods of simplifying accounts for small businesses for tax purposes. Small businesses have yet to be defined but are likely to be businesses with turnover not exceeding the VAT registration limit (£77,000 2012/13) and are likely to exclude limited companies.

Glossary

Every walk of life has its own terminology.
Accounting is no different.

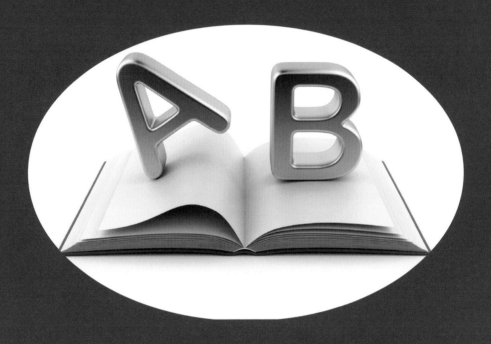

Glossary

ACCOUNTS
A summary of the business financial activities for a period of time, commonly 12 months. They can also be referred to as financial statements. Can be Profit & Loss (Statement of Income and Expenses) or P & L and Balance Sheet

ACCRUALS
Expenses that relate to the accounts but have not yet been billed

ACCRUALS VAT
Accounting for VAT on bills received

ASSETS
Things of value to the business

BUSINESS/TRADE
"Business" is the same as "trade"

CAPITAL ACCOUNT
The profit the business has made not drawn by the owner(s)

NB Could also include loans from the owners

CAPITAL EXPENSES
A payment for something that is going to last

CASH
"Cash" in accountancy terms is used to describe any transaction which is paid immediately however it is paid e.g. with cash or by cheque or debit card, as opposed to transactions which will be paid later i.e. are on credit

CASH ACCOUNTING VAT
Accounting for VAT on bills paid

CASHFLOW STATEMENT
A statement of cash movements that have already happened

CASHFLOW FORECAST
A cashflow forecast is a prediction of future cash movements often month by month

"COMPANY"

The expression "my company" is commonly used to mean any business whether a company or a sole trade or partnership

COMPANY OFFICERS

Company officers are its directors and company secretary (if it has one)

COST OF GOODS SOLD (COGS)

Purchases sold during the year (Opening Stock plus Purchases less Closing Stock). Also, known as Cost of Sales

CREDITORS

The people or organisations the business owes money to. Money owed to suppliers is often referred to as 'Trade Creditors'

CURRENT ASSETS

Cash, money in bank, Debtors, Stock, possibly investments

DEBTORS

The people that owe money to the business

DEPRECIATION

An allowance each year for assets wearing out

DIRECTOR

Officer running a company

DIRECTORS CURRENT OR LOAN ACCOUNT

The record of what the director owes the company or what it owes him

DIVIDENDS

Payments to a company's shareholders

DRAWINGS

Money taken by the owner(s) for themselves e.g. for personal expenditure

FINANCIAL STATEMENTS

Accounts

FIXED ASSETS
Intangible assets e.g. goodwill and tangible assets e.g. property, vehicles, equipment

FIXTURES & FITTINGS
Assets attached to premises

"FIRM"
The word "firm" is often used to describe a partnership

GOODWILL
Good reputation of business that leads to repeat business

GROSS PROFIT
Sales less purchases sold (Cost of Goods Sold)

GROSS PROFIT RATIO
Gross Profit/Sales x 100 to give a percentage

INPUT VAT
VAT on expenses

INVOICES/BILLS
This book tends to use the word "Invoices" when taking about Sales and "Bills" when talking about Expenses

LIABILITIES
Things that the business owes

LONG TERM LIABILITIES
Loans that a business is paying back over more than 1 year

MANAGEMENT ACCOUNTS
Management accounts provide detailed information about different aspects and parts of the business

NOMINALS (Nominal Accounts)
The Categories or mini accounts of Sales, Expenses, etc

OUTPUT VAT
VAT on sales

PROFESSION
People who do jobs which need special training and skill and often involve a high level of education, such as doctors or lawyers

PROVISIONS
Expenses that relate to the accounts but may not arise

RECEIPTS
Receipt for the payment for goods or services such as a till receipt or receipt for something paid in cash

REGISTERED OFFICE
The official address for a company at Companies House

REVENUE EXPENSES
A payment for something that gets used up

SELF EMPLOYED
Being "self employed" means you are your own boss and answer only to yourself

SHARES
The owners stake and share of the company

STOCK
Unsold or unused purchases

VAT
Value Added Tax

WORK IN PROGRESS
Unfinished sales

WRONGFUL TRADING
Trading while unable to pay the business debts

For your own notes

Test Yourself!

What have you learned about accounts and bookkeeping?

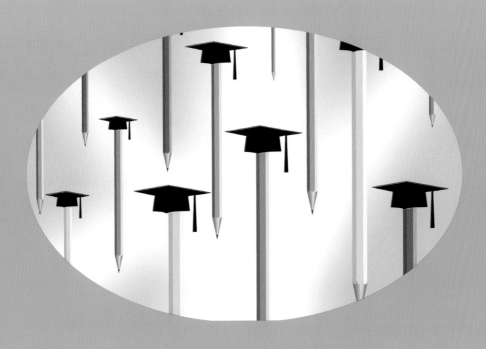

Questions

Check your understanding of this book
Answers on Pages 272 - 281

1. What are the various ways you can be in business?

2. What are accounts?

3. Why might you need accounts?

4. What do you need to prepare accounts?

5. What basic records must you keep?

6. What would simple accounts consist of?

7. What is the single, most important question when preparing accounts?

8. What happens if a business does not keep any records?

9. What makes up a full set of accounts?

10. What does a Balance Sheet tell you that a P & L does not?

11. What do we call customers who have not paid for the goods or services they have had?

12. What do we call the Suppliers the business has not paid?

13. What is a balance sheet?

14. What does the Balance Sheet represent?

15. What 3 main things does a Balance Sheet show?

16. What are assets?

17. What are liabilities?

18. What are Net Assets?

19. Is the owner of the business one and the same as the business or is the owner separate?

20. What is the capital account?

21. What must the Net Assets and Capital Account do?

22. What should a business keep records of?

23. How long must it keep them?

24. What is the core record (though not necessarily a complete record) that a business has?

25. What is the minimum record books you must keep (on a computer or paper)?

26. What should you reference number?

27. What must you note to avoid getting in a muddle?

28. How do you record bills in the Cashbook?

29. What are all the business record books you could keep?

30. What must you pay your employees?

31. Business expenses can be which one of 2 categories?

32. Where are revenue expenses and where do they go in the accounts?

33. What are capital expenses and where do they go in accounts?

34. What is another name for direct costs?

35. What are direct costs?

36. What is Cost of Goods Sold?

37. What is Gross Profit?

38. What is Net Profit?

39. What are indirect costs?

40. What are Accruals?

41. What are Provisions?

42. What are Prepayments?

43. What items appear in both the P & L and the BS?

44. What are the two types of assets?

45. What are Fixed Assets?

46. What are Current Assets?

47. What are the two types of Liabilities?

48. What are Current Liabilities?

49. What are Long Term Liabilities?

50. Why can the bank balance in the balance sheet be different to the bank balance on the bank statements?

51. What does VAT stand for?

52. When do you have to register for VAT?

53. If you have bought something which includes VAT and you are NOT VAT registered, what amount do you enter in your records?

54. If you are VAT registered, you charge VAT on your sales invoices. Is this the VAT you pay to HMRC?

55. What is the VAT on sales invoices called?

56. What is the VAT on purchase invoices called?

57. What are the two ways of calculating VAT?

58. What is Accruals?

59. What is Cash Accounting?

60. When do you pay VAT?

61. Where is VAT shown in the Profit & Loss and Balance Sheet?

62. What is the capital account called in company accounts?

63. What extra things will/might you see in a company's P & L?

64. How do directors/shareholders take their drawings?

65. What are directors of limited companies required to do by law?

66. What must you always have in Double Entry bookkeeping?

67. Illustrate the debit or credit grid that helps you decide what is a debit and what a credit?

68. What is the name in Double Entry for each category?

69. What is made from all the balances on the Nominals prior to preparing the accounts?

70. What must the TB do?

71. What must you give your accountant for him to prepare your accounts?

72. In addition to the above, what could you provide to your accountant to reduce the time he needs to spend preparing your accounts?

73. When must the accounts figures for sole traders and partnerships be submitted to HMRC?

74. What is the tax year (income tax)?

75. When must company accounts be submitted to Companies House?

76. When must company accounts be submitted to HMRC?

77. When must corporation tax be paid to HMRC?

How Did You Do?

Answers to the Questions on Pages 268 - 271

1. What are the various ways you can be in business?

   - Sole trader

   - Partnership

   - Limited Company

   - Limited Liability Partnership

2. What are accounts?

   Accounts are a summary of the business financial activities for a period of time, commonly 12 months (also known as financial statements)

3. Why might you need accounts?

   - To see how the business is doing

   - Where more than one person is running the business, to show their stake in the business

   - To raise money

   - For insurance claims

   - For Tax Returns and for Companies House if the business is a company

   - For selling the business

4. What do you need to prepare accounts?

   Records

5. What basic records must you keep?

   Sales invoices, bills & receipts

6. What would simple accounts consist of?

   Statement of Income and Expenses, or Profit & Loss.

7.   What is the single, most important question when preparing accounts?

What is the period covered by the accounts

8.   What happens if a business does not keep any records?

It can be fined by HMRC

9.   What makes up a full set of accounts?

A Profit & Loss AND a Balance Sheet

10. What does a Balance Sheet tell you that a P & L does not?

- How much you have in the bank
- How much is owed to you
- How much you owe
- The value of vehicles, equipment, etc that you have
- Whether you have any loans or HP outstanding
- Whether there is anything left of the profit the business has made over the years after the money you have taken for yourself.

11. What do we call customers who have not paid for the goods or services they have had?

Debtors

12. What do we call the Suppliers the business has not paid?

Creditors

13. What is a Balance Sheet?

It is a snapshot of what the business is worth on one day

14. What does the Balance Sheet represent?

The balances of every item or category that make up the accounts

15. What are the 3 main things that a Balance Sheet shows?

Assets, Liabilities & Capital Account

16. What are assets?

Things of value belonging to the business e.g. property, equipment, debtors, cash at bank, stock, etc

17. What are liabilities?

Things that the business owes e.g. creditors, loans

18. What are Net Assets?

Assets less liabilities

19. Is the owner of the business one and the same as the business or is the owner separate?

Separate

20. What is the capital account?

It is a record of what the business owes the owner represented by the Net Assets

21. What must the Net Assets and Capital Account do?

Balance

22. What should a business keep records of?

- Sales
- Expenses
- Assets
- Liabilities
- Stock
- Money spent by the owner on himself i.e. drawings
- How everything has been paid e.g. bank, cash or card
- Wages

23.   How long must it keep them?

Under tax law, basically the last 6 tax years

24.   What is the core record (though not necessarily a complete record) that a business has?

Bank statements

25.   What is the minimum record books you must keep (on a computer or paper)?

Cashbook

26.   What should you reference number?

Bills

27.   What must you note to avoid getting in a muddle?

You must note invoices, bills and receipts, how and when they are paid

28.   How do you record bills in the Cashbook?

Either record each invoice and bill and how it is paid OR record each payment and keep invoices/bills together that are paid together

29.   What are all the business record books you could keep?

- Cashbook

- Sales Ledger

- Purchase Ledger

- Nominal Ledger

- Wages Book

- Petty Cash Book

30.   What must you pay your employees?

The National Minimum Wage

31. Business expenses can be one of which 2 categories?

Capital or revenue

32. Where are revenue expenses and where do they go in the accounts?

Revenue expenses are day-to-day expenses and appear in the P & L

33. What are capital expenses and where do they go in accounts?

Capital expenses are one-off expenses and go in the BS

34. What is another name for direct costs?

Purchases

35. What are direct costs?

Costs or expenses that directly relate to producing/selling goods or providing services e.g. goods bought to sell in a shop

36. What is Cost of Goods Sold?

Opening stock plus purchases less closing stock (COGS)

37. What is Gross Profit?

Sales less purchases sold

38. What is Net Profit?

Gross Profit less indirect costs or overheads

39. What are indirect costs

- Employees' Salaries & Wages

- Business premises, including rent, business rates, utility bills (electricity, gas, water)

- Repairs and maintenance of premises and equipment

- Administration such as stationery, postage, telephone and fax, computer, and staff involved in administration, also software

- Insurance

- Advertising & Marketing, Website

- Motor Vehicles

- Staff Travel & Meals (Subsistence) while away on business

- Professional Services e.g. accountants, solicitors

- Finance Interest & Charges e.g. bank overdraft interest and charges

- Miscellaneous Costs such as trade or professional journals or subscriptions

40. What are Accruals?

Unbilled expenses e.g. electricity

41. What are Provisions?

Possible expenses e.g. claims made against the business

42. What are Prepayments?

Expenses paid in advance e.g. rent

43. What items appear in both the P & L and the BS?

Depreciation, Closing Stock, Accruals and Provisions

44. What 2 types of assets are there?

Fixed and Current

45. What are Fixed Assets?

Intangible assets like goodwill or tangible assets like

property, vehicles, equipment, etc with or after depreciation

46.   What are Current Assets?

Trade debtors, stock, cash, money in the bank, and possibly investments

47.   What two types of Liabilities are there?

Current and long term

48.   What are Current Liabilities?

Trade creditors

49.   What are Long Term Liabilities?

Loans

50.   Why can the bank balance in the balance sheet be different to the bank balance on the bank statements?

Because of payments e.g. cheques and/or deposits which have cleared the bank after the balance sheet date

51.   What does VAT stand for?

Value Added Tax

52.   When do you have to register for VAT?

You have to register in the month after your sales or turnover exceed a limit (2012/13 £77,000)

53.   If you have bought something which includes VAT and you are NOT VAT registered, what amount do you enter in your records?

The full amount. You ignore the fact that some is VAT

54.   If you are VAT registered, you charge VAT on your sales invoices. Is this the VAT you pay to HMRC?

No. It is this VAT less the VAT you have paid on things you have bought

55.   What is the VAT on sales invoices called?

Sales or Output VAT

56.   What is the VAT on purchase invoices called?

Purchase or Input VAT

57.   What are the two ways of calculating VAT?

Accruals & Cash Accounting

58.   What is Accruals?

Accruals VAT is accounting for VAT on invoices whether or not they have been paid?

59.   What is Cash Accounting?

Cash accounting VAT is accounting for VAT only on invoices that have been paid?

60.   When do you pay VAT?

Every 3 months, 30 days after the end of your VAT quarter

61.   Where is VAT shown in the Profit & Loss and Balance Sheet?

Nowhere in the P & L. Accounts are prepared exclusive of VAT. Outstanding VAT will appear as a creditor in the BS

62.   What is the capital account called in company accounts?

Reserves/Retained Profits

63.   What extra things will/might you see in a company's P & L?

Tax and dividends

64.   How do directors/shareholders take their drawings?

As a salary, as a dividend(s), or as a loan

65.   What are directors of limited companies required to do by law?

They must run the company for the benefit of all the shareholders, submit annual returns and accounts to

Companies House, and notify Companies House of any changes in the company's officers, registered office and shares

66. What must you always have in Double Entry bookkeeping?

2 transactions, a Debit and a Credit

67. Illustrate the debit or credit grid that helps you decide what is a debit and what is a credit?

Debits	Credits
Expenses	Sales
Assets	Liabilities

68. What is the name in Double Entry for each category?

Nominal account or just nominal

69. What is made from all the balances on the Nominals prior to preparing the accounts?

Trial Balance

70. What must the TB do?

Balance

71. What must you give your accountant for him to prepare your accounts?

- Records including at least a Cashbook, copy VAT and PAYE Returns if applicable

- Stock Listing

72.   In addition to the above, what could you provide to your accountant to reduce the time he needs to spend preparing your accounts?

- A list of the bank transactions that you have included in your figures but which do not appear on the bank statements until after the end of the year e.g. unpresented cheques and reconciliation with the closing bank balance

- A list of debtors and creditors

- A Trial Balance including all cash and bank transactions and debtors and creditors

- Sales listing if not included in the records

73.   When must the accounts figures for sole traders and partnerships be submitted to HMRC?

On Self Assessment Tax Returns by 31st January following the end of the tax year

74.   What is the tax year (income tax)?

6th April to 5th April

75.   When must company accounts be submitted to Companies House?

Normally 9 months after the company's year end

76.   When must company accounts be submitted to HMRC?

Normally 12 months after the company's year end

77.   When must corporation tax be paid to HMRC?

Normally 9 months after the year end

Excerpt from Sage 50 Accounts 2012 in easy steps...

8

Hot tip

Use the demo data provided to fully familiarise yourself with the program before getting started. To do this simply click File, Open from the main menu and select Open Demo Data.

Beware

Some things, once entered, cannot be easily changed. Therefore, make sure you have all the relevant information to hand before using Sage 50 Accounts for the first time.

Don't forget

You can have a go at setting up a company without affecting your actual accounts data by selecting Open Practice Data from the File, Open menu option.

Introduction

All businesses need to keep accurate accounts. If information is not entered correctly, especially when using a computer program, then the accounts will be wrong – you can't blame the computer!

Working through Sage 50 Accounts 2012 in easy steps

This book explains in simple, easy stages how to perform the main tasks required for keeping computerised business accounts. The following chapters show how to:

- Set defaults and Company preferences
- Create customer & supplier records and set up price lists
- Set up opening balances, maintain Bank accounts
- Maintain the Nominal Ledger and run an audit trail
- Generate sales orders and control stock
- Print invoices, credit notes and statements
- Produce history and financial reports

Note: the actual functions available to you will depend on whether you have Sage 50 Accounts, Accounts Plus or Professional. You can even use this book if you work with Sage Instant Accounts.

'Preparing to start' checklist

Before getting started with Sage 50 Accounts 2012, work through the checklist below.

- Check the start date of your company's financial year
- Check with an accountant which VAT scheme is used
- Draw up a list of defaults to use
- Decide on users and passwords
- Back-up the data if updating Sage
- Have customer, supplier and bank details to hand
- Product details, recommend a stock take
- A list of all opening balances

...to introduce you to Sage accounting software

Starting Sage 50

Turn on your computer and wait for the Windows Desktop to appear. To start your Sage 50 program do the following:

1 Click on the Windows Start button.

2 Click on All Programs – a selection appears

3 Click on the Sage Accounts folder

4 Click on Sage 50 Accounts 2012

5 The Sage 50 desktop appears

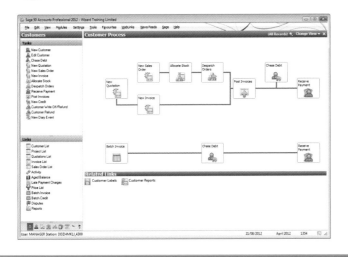

Hot tip

Alternatively, if a shortcut has been set up on the Windows desktop, you can open Sage 50 by double-clicking on the shortcut icon:

Beware

Remember that your reporting will not be accurate until all your opening balances have been entered. Ask your accountant for these, if possible before you start using Sage 50.

Hot tip

You can create multiple delivery addresses so that you can have goods delivered to a number of customer sites whilst specifying a different invoice address.

283

9

ISBN: 978-1-84078-530-2 (£10.99) **Visit www.ineasysteps.com for details or to buy**

Index